Silk Press Books

A division of the Silk Press Ltd

14a Bath Street
Hale
Cheshire WA14 2EJ
Tel. 0161 929 4884 or 0161 928 0333
Fax. 0161 929 8656

Cover design, layout and typesetting
Christine Pemberton

Printed by Redwood Books,
Trowbridge,
Wiltshire BA14 8RM

A WINDOW ON KNUTSFORD

Seven Essays on the History and Architecture of Knutsford

MATTHEW HYDE

The Silk Press
2000

ACKNOWLEDGMENTS

This book was researched during the first half of the year 2000 and written in June and early July, so it is nothing if not immediate. I decided to select a small number of buildings which interested me and follow up the people and events connected with them to see where they took me, rather than making any attempt at a comprehensive story of Knutsford. That is still to be written. Nevertheless it is surprising how the separate places chosen have linked up with each other, and with the world, to build up a picture of this most rewarding town. So this is intended, as Pevsner would say, as a ballon d'essai; seven essays or try-outs for a history and architectural survey of Knutsford.

A book like this cannot be written without generous and friendly help from a lot of people. My thanks are particularly due to Harry H Fairhurst for the sketchbooks of Richard Harding Watt and of his own grandfather Harry S Fairhurst; and to Joan Leach for her help and support. Also to Tim Walton, Pam Upchurch, Kath Goodchild, John Hughes, Graham Holland, Julian Heaton, Mike Willis-Fear, Mick Ricketts, Hazel Hewitt, Pat Heath, Paul and Liz Foden and Ken Latham, Val Brooker, Moira Stevenson, John and Penny Culshaw, Mr and Mrs Macdonald Smith, and to Mr and Mrs Cooper-Baguley and Mrs Gasparini and Terry Jones; to Margaret Winstanley and Jacques of Toc H and Mr Geoffrey Booth, to Jeremy Milln, Chris Crowe and Peter de Figueiredo, to Helen Perry and Jackie Heaton at Knutsford library.

Matthew Hyde

CONTENTS

One
TATTON OLD HALL

The roof - the Battle of Bosworth 1485 - Sir William Stanley - Lady Margaret Beaufort - the Stanley style - Sir William's other holdings and works. The Old Hall interpreted. James Stanley vicar of Rostherne - his life and works - Manchester cathedral. The New Hall and the Park - 18th century landscaping - the lost village of Tatton. The Old Hall and Tatton Park in WW2 - and today.

Tatton Old Hall today is an unprepossessing sight, situated in low ground at the head of Tatton Mere among the tumps and bumps of its vanished village, clad in an unattractive red brick with many blocked windows and bowed under its heavy stone roof. It is a site of great antiquity however, settled from the earliest times, and the old house hides one great glory - a magnificent roof. High overhead in the smoky gloom of the great hall, hard to see, and considerably damaged and truncated, the roof is nevertheless a structure of great splendour, richly decorated. It is the presence this roof which links this frowsty old mansion with mainstream history, a rousing chapter in the history of our land when the last of the Plantagenet kings was defeated in battle at Bosworth Field and the victorious Henry Tudor ushered in the cruel dynasty of the Tudors. This was the brief time when Tatton was held by Sir William Stanley, veteran of Bosworth, master of Flint castle and of Holt and Wrexham, and younger brother of the first Lord Derby.

Sir William Stanley

Bosworth Field, 1485. The King of just two year's reign, Richard III, faced the challenger Henry Tudor. Richard held the high ground, and here on top of the hill still floats his royal banner, the boar on a red and blue ground. Down below at the edge of the wood is the standard of Henry Tudor, bearing the Welsh dragon for Henry was born a Welshman. Richard held the stronger position and had mustered the greater force; but the balance of power lay elsewhere, for over to the right, in the stubble fields, there floats a third banner with the distinctive device of the Eagle and Child. Here were gathered the forces of the Stanleys, Lord Thomas and his brother William. Effectively kings of the northwest, the Stanleys were the unknown factor, owing allegiance to both sides. Which way would they turn?

Stanley's position was an unenviable one. His son, George Lord Strange, was held hostage for his loyalty by Richard, but his wife, the formidable Margaret Beaufort, was the widow of Edmund Tudor, Earl of Richmond, and mother of Henry Tudor.

The course of the battle was close, so close that no definitive account of events came out of it. People are still happily arguing about it, not just what exactly happened but who was the villain? Was Richard really the ogre that Shakespeare painted? It seems clear however that the outcome of the fight was undecided until at the last the Stanleys threw their lot in with Henry. The impetuous Sir William charged with his men into the battle when he saw that the Tudor standard bearer, Sir Charles Brandon had been slain. So saving Henry's life. It was he who picked up the crown of England from the thorn bush where it had fallen from the stricken brow of King Richard, but his elder brother Lord Thomas Stanley was the one who actually placed it on the victorious Henry's head, so hailing him as the new king of England. Thomas was rewarded by being created Earl of Derby. William, although rewarded with lands and titles, never received the recognition he felt he deserved for it seems Henry, despite owing his life to William, never fully trusted him.

Shakespeare edited out poor William Stanley, perhaps feeling that his cast list was long enough with just one Stanley, the future Earl of Derby. It was William's fate to be edited out of history.

There has always been a tiresome "Shakespeare couldn't have written Shakespeare" faction, but it is interesting to note that a persistent candidate for that honour is Will Stanley. Not our Will Stanley but an Elizabethan one, the sixth Earl of Derby. If true this would give a new slant to this particular play.

And so with the coronation of Henry VII a new royal dynasty, the House of Tudor, ruled the land. The power behind the new king, as behind the Stanley clan who had placed him on the throne, was Lady Margaret Beaufort, Countess of Richmond. She lies today in demure piety in Westminster Abbey where she died, in the Abbot's house, on St Peter's day 1509. Her monument is an accurate summary of her place in history, for although she appears as a medieval woman of simple piety her bronze effigy is by Pietro Torrigiani, friend and sometimes enemy of Michaelangelo and the first bringer of the pure spirit of the Renaissance to Britain; and her quiet memorial stands within the sumptuous virtuosity of her son's chapel, Henry VII's, the dynastic mausoleum of the Tudors. She was a remarkable woman, of fine intellect and severe conscience and a pioneer of the new learning, who can be credited with a great number of beneficent works. She was the founder of both St John's and Christ's colleges at Cambridge - her arms appear on both the gatehouses - and she endowed the chair of Divinity for her friend and confessor Erasmus. Here in the northwest there are many churches displaying the Stanley style in their architecture, all of them directly or indirectly linked to the Lady Margaret. One work which is thought to have been a direct gift of hers is the angel orchestra of Manchester Cathedral; fourteen superbly carved and near life sized heavenly musicians with outspread wings, each playing a different contemporary instrument, but so difficult to see clearly in the relative darkness of the nave roof.

The Stanleys were great builders, giving thanks for their new-found wealth and status in a string of churches in Lancashire and especially in North Wales. There are signs that, with a Welshman on the throne of England, there was a feeling of greater openness to English influence; so the Welsh churches exhibit a Cheshire style quite different to the local vernacular in their tall battlemented

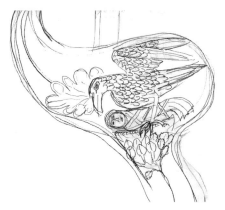

clerestories, flat roofs, wide windows and lavish decoration. Sometimes there is a distinctive three-sided apse. Stanley churches are always signed. The emblems to look for are the Eagle and Child, the eagle's foot caboshed, the three legs of Man, and the hart's head. In the carved bosses or panels of the roof, in bench ends or misericords, in stained glass if it has survived, on corbels and borne on shields by angels, these emblems will appear though they may take some finding. Holt and Gresford, Wrexham and Mold are all Stanley churches, and so is the beautiful well chapel at Holywell, and St Cybi's at Holyhead. In Lancashire, Ormskirk and especially the collegiate church at Manchester, now the cathedral, are connected with the Stanleys; and in Cheshire the Savage chapel at Macclesfield. The connection in this last example is Catherine Stanley, sister to Lord Derby and Sir William. She lies there in superb alabaster elegance, still holding the hand of her husband Sir John Savage, who commanded the left wing of Henry Tudor's army at Bosworth.

It is not too fanciful to suggest that the culmination of the Stanley series is Henry VII's fantastic chapel at Westminster Abbey, which is both the climax of medieval gothic architecture and the point at which it was clear that it had gone about as far as it could go. Here lies Henry himself in gilded magnificence with his queen, Elizabeth of York, the Tudor Arms at their feet supported by Renaissance putti; Torrigiani again.

Contemporary secular works associated with the Stanleys are much harder to recognise and have suffered badly in later times. The Stanley stronghold at Lathom in Lancashire is no more, for it was utterly destroyed in the civil war, and Knowsley is greatly altered. Sir William's pentagonal castle at Holt, where he was reputed to have held vast reserves of gold and jewels, is now just a strange lump of red rock, although the handsome river bridge, built or rebuilt in his time, is still in daily use. His castle at Flint is a melancholy ruin on the desolate sands of Dee. It is only at the manor of Tatton in Cheshire gained through the marriage of his son, also William, to Joan Massey, and that of Weaver Hall through the marriage of his daughter Jane to Sir John Warburton, that we can see the Stanley style in domestic mode.

The glory of Sir William Stanley was to be a short one. He was arrested by an ungrateful monarch in 1494, and beheaded on Tower Hill on the 16th of February 1495. He paid the price of the Stanley's reputation for changing sides and specifically for his possible part in the Perkin Warbeck rebellion; it is known that he felt passed over, always in his brother's shadow, when the rewards for Bosworth were granted, although he was created Lord Chamberlain and a Knight of the Garter as well as constable of the Royal castles of Beaumaris and Caernarvon. I suspect that he was an early victim, with his great personal wealth, of that cupidity and ruthlessness which came to be a Tudor characteristic. It was dangerous to be rich, and was to be even more so in the time Henry VIII.

The Hall Interpreted

Tatton Old Hall is not an easy house to interpret. Medieval great houses generally follow a pattern which makes it possible to understand them, even if much-altered or truncated. The great hall is the nucleus; open to the roof to allow the smoke of the hearth to rise and escape, and with the high table of the lord and lady of the manor at one end and the outer doors at the other. There were always two doors opposite one another with a passageway between them; this is one feature to look for when interpreting an old house because it identifies the high end and the low end. The passageway is called the screens because it needed to be. Here in the northwest it is usually screened by bringing in a partition to a pair of posts, called speres, a yard or so in from the outer walls; and sometimes by a screen as well, supposedly movable, in between the spere posts. The spere truss and screen would be highly decorated, as can be seen at Rufford and formerly at Salmesbury in Lancashire. There is a plainer but excellent example with a screen in Manchester at Chetham's, and a good complete example, but without a screen, at Ordsall in Salford.

Cross wings were added at the two ends of the great hall to make an H-shape. At the high end, behind the high table, was the family wing with parlour below and solar above. The other end was the service wing, with a buttery and pantry side-by-side and a passage between them leading to the kitchen, which in case of fire was outside the main structure. These three were often given three matching or graduated doorways; so the screens passage could be quite a showpiece altogether.

Here at Tatton it is difficult to fit the old building into the pattern. It is not H-shaped but L-shaped - just one long wing and the great hall. One wing must be missing; which one? Entry into the hall is next to the blank end wall. That would make this the low end. In which case it must be the kitchen wing, at the low end, which is missing.

Wrong. It is more tricky than that. A nice puzzle in standing archaeology in fact. Unfortunately there is no evidence for a doorway in the opposite wall, nor can any sign be seen of spere posts which would mark a screens passage. But if you look up at the other end of the splendid roof, where the gallery is now, there are deep empty mortice holes in the underside of the penultimate tie beam. One of the pleasures of interpreting a timber-framed building is that the remaining pieces always tell you where there have been bits taken away. So something big has been taken away here; two big bits in fact, each about a yard in from the side walls. Also this last bay is wider than all the others.

Explanation:- this was the screens passage, the missing pieces are the spere posts.

The original doors must have been lost when the side walls were built away.

Now a puzzle is explained. You might expect to get a better view of the carved decoration of the roof from the gallery. It is disappointing to find that this is not so, because it all faces the other way. Of course; we are looking from the low end. The decoration faces the other way, towards the high table which stood, after all, roughly where the modern recreated one is.

But not quite. The roof seems to end very abruptly at the end wall above the high table, and on the outside of this wall can be seen the decayed remains of a truss with empty mortice holes facing thin air. So it is evident that the great hall has been cut short. It was longer by at least one more bay, possibly two. This makes sense, because the carved decoration of the roof is only visible today in extreme foreshortening. When the hall was longer you could get further back and see it much better.

But whether there ever was a second cross-wing at this end is doubtful. No trace of one has ever been found. Although the H-shape with two wings was the commonest arrangement sometimes one cross-wing sufficed, making a T shape. Chorley Hall at Alderley Edge is like this. Service accommodation is below and a family solar above, reached by a spiral stair. The stair was given its own doorway in the screens, making four in a row instead of the usual three; which is pretty spectacular.

No attempt is made here at interpreting the long cross-wing at Tatton although it is clearly of great interest, preserving its roofs and internal partitions of timber but with the outer walls built away in brick presumably at the same time as the great hall was done.

In the spring of 2000, before the old hall reopened to the public, the inside walls were washed and scraped of their limewash preparatory to repainting. It was possible then to ascend the wobbly scaffold towers and examine some of the timbers of the roof at close range. The oddest thing is that the carved decoration of vine trails and leaves is all applied. It is all on planks which are faced onto the main timbers. It is possible that the decorative vertical struts between the braces and the collars, and the frills in between them, are an addition too. So it appears that a fine and sophisticated roof, whose decoration was confined to the structure in the approved fashion - quatrefoil braces and moulded principles - was given a frothy top-dressing to jazz it up. It makes one wonder whether it was done for a particular occasion. Could it have been the marriage, in about 1490, of William Stanley, son of Sir William, and Joan Massey of Tatton and Worsley? I wonder too if it was all once coloured, as the angels of Lady Margaret's heavenly orchestra at Manchester cathedral undoubtedly were.

James Stanley

After the untimely demise of Sir William it is nice to be able to record that another Stanley, James his nephew, was priest of Rostherne - which included Tatton and Knutsford - from 1498 until his translation to Bishop of Ely in 1506. James Stanley was the Warden of the Collegiate church in Manchester, today's cathedral. He set in train the rebuilding of that great church along typical Stanley lines, with its tall lantern clerestorey and highly decorative flat roofs. He was responsible for the wonderful and justly famous choir stalls; his own Warden's stall, now the Dean's, is carved with the Stanley Eagle and Child legend no less than three times over.

I am fond of James Stanley, if it is possible to be fond of a prelate who has been dead these five hundred years. His character, more than that of Sir William, comes through after all this time. He was a warrior priest, standing six foot four. He fought at the battle of Flodden Field in 1513, manfully wielding a mace because a priest was not permitted to bear a sword. He was the father of three children by a lady who was *'not his sister, but who wanted nothing to make his wife save the marriage service'*. The Pope placed him under a ban for his transgressions. At his death in 1525 he directed that he should be buried not at Ely but in his beloved church at Manchester, but because of the Papal displeasure he had to be buried outside the walls on the north side. But his son John circumvented this by causing a chapel to be thrown out to enclose his tomb, and so he came to rest within his church after all. This is not the end of the story however, because this chapel, the Ely chapel, was destroyed in the blitz of 1940 and not rebuilt when the rest of the cathedral was repaired. His memorial brass, showing him splendidly attired as bishop, was rescued from the rubble and remounted in the Stanley chapel. And his body? Who knows, but perhaps it is out in the cold again.

'Of your charity' asks his inscription *'pray for the soul of James Stanley, sometime Bishop of Ely and Warden of the College of Manchester, which departed out of this transitory world the XXII day of March in the year of our Lord MDXXV'.*

Warden Stanley's works at Manchester must have cost an enormous sum. There is some evidence that the king himself contributed to them, perhaps in expiation for the execution of Sir William. The king came to Manchester in June 1495, after visiting in royal state his mother the Lady Margaret and her son, his half-brother the Earl, at Lathom and Knowsley. Warden Stanley's own stall at Manchester has handrests carved with the Eagle and Child on one side and the Stanley Hart on the other. The next one along however is very curious. It is literally two-faced, showing on the far side a jester in motley with bells. This may relate to a Stanley legend, that when the king was at Lathom he was taken up by Lord Thomas onto the leads to survey the country round about. The jester, seeing the king in such a vulnerable position and Lord Thomas at his elbow, whispered in the Earl's ear *"Tom, remember Will"*. The fool was ever after aggrieved that the opportunity for revenge was not taken.

The New Hall and the Park

The story of Tatton Old Hall can be briefly brought up to date, consisting as it does mostly of a slow fall from grace. After the fall of Sir William Stanley his son, also Sir William, was stripped of most of his lands and titles but retained Tatton. However he died in 1498 aged only 26. His wife Joan married twice more and on her death Tatton passed to her only daughter, Joan Stanley. The name of Egerton first appears two generations later with the

marriage of Dorothy to Richard Egerton of Ridley. It was a childless marriage but an illegitimate half-brother, Thomas Egerton 'the Chancellor' bought the reversion in 1598, establishing 350 years of Egerton rule at Tatton.

At some stage in the 17th century a new house was established in a drier and more commanding situation at the north end of the estate. This is the house we know today as Tatton, although its evolution into its present chaste neo-Classical form was a gradual one. The old hall, hidden away in a fold of the ground, was suffered to remain, divided up and lived in by estate staff. When the ancient timber walls rotted, as they do especially at ground level, they were built away in brick. At the same time the open great hall, which was redundant, was floored over to make three stories. It must have been a great surprise, before these floors were removed again in the 1970s, to come across the magnificent open roof of the hall in the attic of an apparently quite humble dwelling, especially as it could all then be seen at close range.

All around Tatton Old Hall is the rolling parkland which is the essential setting for an English Country House. With its wild animals peacefully roaming free in a perfect Arcadian landscape it looks like a last remnant of a lost paradise, when all the rest of the world outside the Park wall was cut up into fields and farms and roads and towns. Not so. Tatton Park was an artful and an effortful creation, requiring the removal of miles of field boundaries, re-routing of roads, eviction and re-housing of tenants, tree-planting on an heroic scale and complicated water engineering. The entire village of Tatton which stood just to the west of the Old Hall was destroyed, leaving just a few mounds and hollows to mark its passing. The whole was then walled and gated to make a private paradise.

Tatton Park & Old Hall in World War Two

The private paradise of the Egertons was unceremoniously invaded during the emergency of World War Two, and the Park saw extraordinary activity especially around the Old Hall. Ringway airport was selected for training in the relatively new technique of parachuting, and the main landing ground, just a few miles to the south, (as we know to our discomfort today), was Tatton. Here was sufficient open space and suitable terrain. Maurice, Lord Egerton, remained in residence, keeping a beady eye on the goings on and trying to balance the demands of the war effort with the preservation of his inheritance - to which we probably owe the survival of the mansion and park in a reasonable state, when so many others emerged from army occupation fit only for breakup and demolition. Maurice, 'Lordy' as he was locally known, treated all the hundreds of evacuees, land girls, paratroopers, officers and men as tiresome but necessary guests.

The Old Hall itself was used for a while as an ammunition store, which did not please

Lord Egerton at all when he found out. He fired off numerous letters of complaint about the damages to his property, whether it was cigarette burns on the furniture or prize rhododendrons uprooted by a crashing bomber. The military authorities must have found him a confounded nuisance, or words to that effect, but perhaps a few understood that his loyalties were torn between patriotism in the great war of nations and the feudal duty of protecting his own little kingdom.

and today

Maurice the fourth and last Baron Egerton of Tatton died in 1958, in Kenya. He directed that his ashes should be scattered to the four winds - so what lies underneath his tomb slab in the grassy churchyard at Rostherne? Unmarried and having no child, he bequeathed his Mansion House Tatton Hall together with the outbuildings and appurtenances thereto and the gardens and pleasure grounds thereof but excluding the Park therewith to the National Trust. As it stood, at 54 acres, this was an unviable proposition for the Trust, but in lieu of the enormous taxes that were due the whole of the home estate of 2000 acres came to the Trust. Lord Egerton had expressed the wish that the Park, and Rostherne Mere, be preserved intact for the benefit of the nation. The Park was without endowment for its maintenance however, so it is managed and run by Cheshire County Council under the watchful eye of the Trust.

The Cloud came to the Trust at the same time. This distinctive hill with a bite out of it where it has been quarried away was where Lord Egerton carried out his radio experiments.

Today Tatton Old Hall is displayed as an educational facility with rooms furnished in different periods. The great hall, its floors removed and the central fire filling it with pungent woodsmoke, is mocked up to resemble its medieval self.

The Old Hall is a leisurely but not particularly short walk through the park from Knutsford; the park bestowing its own particular magic on the way. A great park such as this has such a strong sense of identity that it can survive essentially unchanged the demise of the family that created it, transfer to public ownership, and be run by committee. To enter the park is still, just as much as it ever was, to enter a little kingdom. Different rules apply. People and animals coexist in unusual amity. Priority is given to bikes and deer. Our feet, instead of being directed along narrow hard paths are free to roam where they will on the springy turf. Even the phones are dodgy, as they might be in a far country. The County Council is very proactive, even aggressive, in promoting the park as a venue for events of all sorts. Sometimes these are huge, like the RHS Garden Festival which was held here for the first time in 1999. The park seems to be able to absorb all this and be its usual tranquil self after all the portaloos have departed. Tatton Park is a very major regional asset; to be treasured.

Model reconstruction of Tatton as it might have been at an early stage. Note the screens passage in the centre.

...arved roof, Tatton Old ...all. This photograph and ...e drawing opposite show ...e timbers of the hall roof ... close range before the ...termediate floors were ...ken out.
Courtesy English Heritage

Tatton Old Hall and the imported barn.

The author demonstrates the de Trafford Crest - 'Now Thus' - with a flail, outside the barn at Tatton.

utton Weaver Hall. The
xterior betrays nothing of
e rich medieval interior.

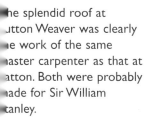

he splendid roof at
utton Weaver was clearly
e work of the same
aster carpenter as that at
atton. Both were probably
ade for Sir William
tanley.

Examples of Stanley work at Manchester Cathedral.
See pages 12 and 13.

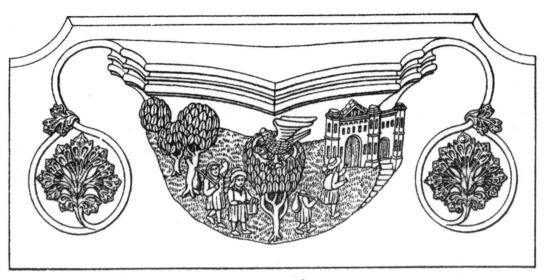

·DECANVS·

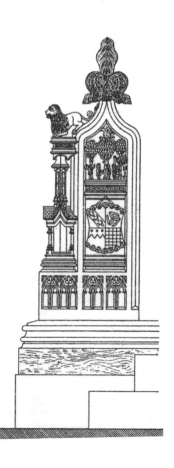

Above: Stanley emblems at Mold church - the Eagle and Child, the Eagle's foot and the three Legs of Man.

Below left: Wrexham church typifies the Stanley style in North Wales. Flat roofs with battlements and pinnacles, tall clerestory, wide nave windows, no division between the nave and chancel and three-sided apse.

Below right: Derby and Ely Chapels, Manchester Cathedral

...int Castle, deserted now ...ve for the ravens, was ...nce Sir William Stanley's ...ronghold.

...uthin church has very ...ne ceilings of typical ...tanley style. Look for ...he Eagle and Child.

Holt in North Wales was the stronghold of Sir William Stanley (see pages 7 and 8).
Of the pentagonal castle little is left, but the bridge and church, complete with Stanley emblems, survive.

The font in Holt church bears the Stanley stag.

Below: Ground plan and engraving of Holt Castle.

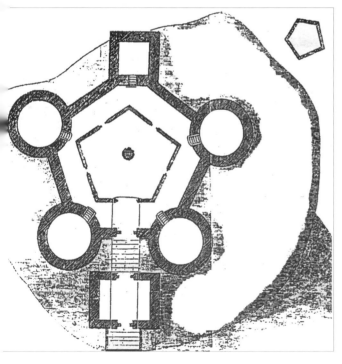

This well-known photograph is very evocative of the war years at Tatton. Maurice, Lord Egerton, in typical down-at-heel dress, with a smart American officer.

'...ly Hupp Car' from Lord
...gerton's album. It is
...aded up with tusks and
...ins.

*Courtesy Manchester
Museum*

...owadays on safari
...e we usually shoot with a
...amera.
...ord Egerton shot first
...nd photographed later, as
...is dead Bontebok bears
...itness.

*Courtesy Manchester
Museum*

A page from Lord Egerton's game book shows meticulous attention to detail.

Kneelers in Rostherne church commemorate the paratroopers at Tatton.

...rd Egerton's African Hut
Tatton.

...ourtesy Knutsford Guardian

AS REPORTED IN KNUTSFORD GUARDIAN DATED FEBRUARY 20TH 1958

An epitaph to "Lordy" by Mr Leslie Hewitt, 12 Springwood Avenue, Shaw Heath (a
married man with four children)

> *What can I write about this man, this man so few men knew,*
>
> *What can I say & in my saying know what I say is true,*
>
> *With his hand upon my shoulder, I remember as a boy,*
>
> *He gave me all his park land to use as my own toy,*
>
> *Well! not exactly gave it - lent it - let us say,*
>
> *But I love our Lordy dearly for ever - for that day,*
>
> *He was a man who loved in life the very simple things,*
>
> *And knew the inner happiness that boyish laughter brings,*
>
> *Yet for all his wealth he sometimes looked so sad,*
>
> *As if he would give his millions - for a boy to call him 'Dad'*
>
> *'Lordy' in your going, goes a fragment of my heart,*
>
> *For as a boy I loved you - yes - loved you from the start,*
>
> *Like your old cloth cap and crumpled mac, your ways were never gaudy,*
>
> *May you rest in peace & know one thing; You will be remembered 'Lordy'.*

TWO
KING STREET

A critical walk from the railway bridge to the Tatton Gate - return studying a few buildings in detail - the old vicarage and Alison Uttley - Henry Antrobus - the Patisserie surveyed - Drs Holland - the Legh of Booths' town house? - Brook Street chapel - summary

'Here was England, neither north nor south, nor east nor west; but England unqualified and unconditioned, slow to receive strangers, placidly polite, caring nothing as to what they thought of it, ashamed as to any curiosity concerning their indubitably improper intentions. Knutsford had, moreover, a high street and a low street. The first boasted its name, the second would have repudiated it; but, between the High Street and the Low, little lanes of understanding ran up and down in a wayward but attractive manner. Here indeed was the Church of England itself set forth in solid parable.'
(*Plain Tales from Flanders* - see the chapter on the Sessions House and Gaol)

This was PB 'Tubby' Clayton's first impression of Knutsford in January 1919.

King Street, or Bottom Street as it is more descriptively but less politely known, is very satisfactory, with a nice curve to it so that it doesn't reveal too much at once.

Starting at the bottom of Bottom Street, by the railway bridge and heading north, it is at first pleasantly cottagey and relatively uneventful. There are a few taller Georgian houses, and then the churchyard wall opposite the site of the old chapel of ease. On the left is Bailey's cafe, a good early timber-framed building running back up the hill in characteristic medieval fashion, but the low block of shops opposite, revealing little of their equally ancient timbering within, runs parallel with the street. It is worth looking for datestones on King Street; a chunky brick house with a fat chimney follows Bailey's, carrying the date 1721 and the initials JMH. The narrow pavement was the gift of Lady Jane Stanley; hers was the last sedan chair, which still has an annual outing in the May Day parade. Lady Stanley's gift to the town was tempered by her moral sense, for she did not like to see young women and men walking out together, so she made it necessary to walk in single file.

At the midpoint is the punctuation mark of the Belle Epoque with its tall white tower, a very quirky building - see the Watt chapter - propped up on each side by a showy black-and-white pub. Both the pubs are rebuilds of ancient inns. Soon afterwards is the Royal George Hotel, formerly the George and

Dragon, which fully lives up to its grand name, opposite which is a group of three good 17th/early 18th century houses, to which we will be returning. The next building to catch the eye is number 101, on an island site in front of the old marketplace, red and white with the oriel windows made fashionable by Norman Shaw's New Zealand Chambers in London. Opposite that a couple of narrow entries lead into interesting yards, one containing the Heritage Centre, an old smithy, and the next the courtyard cafe, hung with pennyfarthings. From these yards the ancient town layout of long narrow burgage plots running back from the street is very evident, with the roof lines following the plots back from the gabled frontages. The White Lion is an excellent example. Now the shops stop, giving way to solicitors, and the street finishes with a fine architectural flurry. Two admirable coaching inns, the Angel and its counterpart opposite, sometimes called the Marble Arch, follow, then the old Post Office, which has been given the Watt treatment - see the sundial and the side balcony. On the left is the Tatton agent's house, rather grave, facing a very Mancunian-looking Victorian bank in orange brick, hard Derbyshire stone and polished granite, with lots of architectural tricks. It has acquired a Mediterranean garden in front. Finally on the right an unequal pair of early 18th century houses, one tallish and plain, the other small but cheeky. They face some good small modern flats and a final row of cottages.

Now comes the surprise.

The bothersome traffic is led away and King Street turns into a gently curved and shaded path, gradually revealing the grand entrance archway to Tatton Park. The effect when you become aware of the vast open parkland beyond in contrast to the confined and busy street is stunning. It was a very carefully contrived effect, which we have equally carelessly thrown away by putting up a plethora of signs; I counted thirteen of them, including an enormous and bright blue KEEP LEFT sign placed exactly where it does the most visual damage, straight through the archway. Repton would weep.

The Old Vicarage

From the Tatton Park end the very first house on the left has a blue plaque, telling us that it was given as a Vicarage in 1718, and that the children's author and countrywoman Alison Uttley lived here for a while c1910. It is moreover the sweetest little house, very Dutch with its brick pilasters and its air of importance at odds with its diminutive size.

Alison Uttley was a prolific writer of children's stories, of which the Little Grey Rabbit books were strong favourite with children of a pedantic bent; much more wordy than Beatrix Potter and with fussy illustrations by Margaret Tempest, but published in an equally cute format. This is what Alison Uttley had to say about the house :-

'The first real house which I had the felicity of

helping to find was the Old Vicarage, where I lived when I was married (which was in 1911). It was a whitewashed seventeenth-century house with panelled sitting rooms, and oak shutters to cover the windows and keep out the cold. There were cupboards in the thickness of the walls, and tiny cupboards over the beds to hold a book and a candlestick. A beautiful staircase with newels at each turn, went from the cellars to the big attic, which had once been the council chamber for the town. It was the house where Peter lived in Mrs Gaskell's "Cranford".'

So it is. This is from her book of essays 'Plowman's Clocks' 1952. Mrs Uttley was always very sensitive to the atmosphere of an old house, as anyone who has read her 'A Traveller in Time' will know.

'I was aware of warmth and sweetness and good fellowship, but after the shutters had been fastened across the windows, and the candles lighted, the rooms were dim as if no fires or lights could dispel the ghosts who lived there. In the daytime it was gay and bright and lively, the cobbled streets of the old town echoed with footsteps, with the whistling of boys and the clatter of horses' hooves at 'The Angel'. On May Day there was a May Queen, and the procession moved through the streets under my windows. Yet after a year of happiness we had to leave this house and for some years had no settled home.'

In a later book of essays, 'Wild Honey' 1962, she gives us a lot more atmosphere and a bit more detail :-

'The house was seventeenth century and this cellar was admired by everyone who saw it as a romantic place. We reached it by a carved oak staircase with fine balusters which had square newels at the corners, and broad shallow steps which led down from the hall. A little green door with glass panels led off the cellar stairs to the garden, half-way down, and then we continued, holding the smooth seventeenth-century oak handrail to the bottom, where we walked on stone floors and entered the rooms. They had been used as a garden room, a wash-house and a wine-cellar. They were fresh and clean and bright in the sunshine, whitewashed and painted green, and lighted by windows. Who would have guessed how sinister the cellars would look in a cataract of moonlight? What kind of face might appear against the window glass of the door to the garden? A face of 'crumpled linen' might easily look in. What might lurk in those underground rooms, what spectre from the house's ancient past when the Cranford ladies had knocked at that very door? Who might step lightly up the flight of stairs, appearing round the corner where the staircase turned at right angles? What ghost from another century would walk there? I was alarmed and I was silent, for the house was not silent. Little feet of mice scampered about down there and groans came from the timbers. The house was lighted by gas but the cellars and passages had nothing to illuminate them, so I carried a candle and the long shadows dipped and curtseyed and shot up to the ceiling and fell to the stairway as my hand shook. Every night there was an ordeal to go upstairs and to come down from my bedroom, to pass the corner of the broad stairway which led down to the

cellars, where who-knows-what were having high jinks down below. In a flash something might scuttle up the stairs and seize me. I was often alone till late at night and I sat in the panelled little parlour reading or playing the piano, unwilling to pass that open stairway.

Yet nothing came up the stairs, no ghost appeared, only whispers and sighs and gentle murmurs which made my hair stand on end and my cheeks turn scarlet as I took up my candle and went up the stairs, determined to put my fears to flight.'

After the expectations raised by its fine front, and especially after reading this, to step inside the Old Vicarage today is a grave disappointment. Where is the panelling, where the oak stair? Come to that where are the plaster cornices and panelled doors? It is all gone. The house was stripped out completely in about 1964 when it was converted to offices, and all that is left inside is the basic disposition of the rooms and stairwell. It is clear that Mrs Uttley's recollections were accurate, for the stairway is wide and straight, and runs from the cellars to the attic, with a door to the garden midway down to the cellar indeed; but it is all modern. We can only be grateful for her description because it appears to be the only record of what is gone.

Alison Uttley was more interesting than, but not as nice, as her Grey Rabbit books would lead one to suppose. Born on a farm near Cromford in Derbyshire she made her way to Grammar school in Bakewell and then to the new university of Manchester where she read physics, being only the second female graduate in that discipline. From there life took her to Cambridge and London, and then to live here in Knutsford for a short time and then Bowdon, and finally to Beaconsfield in the Chilterns, where she was a somewhat hostile neighbour of Enid Blyton. The curious thing is that her imaginative life, the source of all her voluminous writings, remained utterly fixed on that Country Childhood in Derbyshire; but she did not feel the need to return there, neglecting her aging parents and scarcely even recording the existence of her brother. It is also salutary to record that the creator of the cosy Little Grey Rabbit and the comical Sam Pig had the most tragic family life, for her husband committed suicide and so, eventually, did their only son.

'I am drowning myself in the Mersey below the bridge' wrote James Uttley in his suicide note, left in his office. James was in charge of building a new bridge for Manchester Corporation at Northenden and drowned himself there on the 18th of September 1930.

'My family held the view that James was allowed no peace at home, that he was driven to drown himself through worrying about money and constant nagging by Alison' wrote Martin Byers in 1984, on the suicide of James Uttley.

Rylands Library, Deansgate, holds the Alison Uttley archive including a box of revealing photographs. She was a strong-looking woman, perhaps too strong, with dark eyes and an English-rose complexion even into old age. Had she not found her fulfilment in writing she would have been a formidable leader and organiser. Her father Henry Taylor looks very much the countryman, with a fringe of hair and beard, thumbs in waistcoat pocket, a shrewd and challenging look and a stance so upright that he seems to lean backward slightly. Charles Tunnicliffe captured him well in the woodcuts that illustrate her essays. Her mother Hannah, small and slightly pop-eyed, tends in photographs to stand in her husband's shadow. She looks as though she would be very soft-spoken but not to be ignored; a little unbalanced - but that may be just hindsight.

The Heritage Centre

A few yards along King Street and across the road a narrow entry leads to the Heritage Centre. Behind the shops that line the street is small timber-framed building standing in a yard. No doubt there were once many such small workshops tucked away behind the street front. It was a blacksmith's shop - the forge is still there and the great bellows now displayed on the stairs was found in situ. From the front yard it is possible to see an archway, now blocked, that would have given better access off the street than the present passageway.

It is a simple post and rail frame of two bays with square panels, indicating a useful rather than ornamental building of late date, probably 17th or even 18th century. But clearly it was ruinous, and the reconstruction has been so thorough that little more can be said. When the timbers are in place they can tell you by their joints what is missing, even if there is hardly anything left. I recall helping to survey a tiny hall near Alderley where the timbers of one side had all been built away in brick, leaving just a part of the timber wall plate under the eaves. Even so it was possible to reconstruct the lost frame from the empty mortice and peg holes. But when the timbers have been moved, as here, their evidence cannot be trusted.

A fine staircase has been incorporated in the rebuild which doesn't belong here at all but in a building of much higher status. It would be nice to know its story. This would have had a simple ladder of some sort, perhaps just a vertical plank with footholes, supplementing the external stair at the back.

From the blacksmith's yard the ancient way in which Knutsford was built up on this side of King Street is very clear to see. On either side are the rear gables of the timber-framed houses that would have lined the street once, giving it a zig-zag profile. Most have been refronted in Georgian brick or rebuilt entirely, with level parapets hiding the roofs. The plots stretch right back to the top street - typical long, narrow burgage plots - and sometimes the houses stretch back a long way too, like the White Lion on the next plot but one. Between the plots are even narrower alleys - some now blocked or petering out but many still in use. It looks as though the old blacksmith's shop occupies the yards of two burgage plots.

The next port of call, opposite the Royal George, is

The Patisserie

This is a building that attracted me first by its cakes and then by the splendidly wide oak staircase, clearly by its chunkiness late 17th century, and particularly by the fact that this staircase leads downwards to the cellar floor, where something utilitarian would be expected.

Patisserie 37 Jan 00
Oak, stripped.

I was anticipating that a building of this type would be anonymous, that we would be very unlikely to track down its date other than by the evidence of its style and construction, and even more unlikely to identify its builder. Such however proves not to be the case. In the library, stashed away in the basement along with a few packing cases and one or two other historical relics, is an old lead hopper and downpipe belonging to this house. Not a standard utilitarian item but a fine example of the plumber's art, with a running vine design embossed on the square downpipe and the florid initials and date HA 1697 on the hopper. This would have been right in the middle of the street frontage, between the two dormers.

HA was Henry Antrobus. As luck would have it a broken fragment of his equally florid gravestone turned up while this book was in preparation. The Borough Council carried out some improvements and clearing at the site of the old parochial chapel of St Helen's, which was attended by an archaeological watching brief. Surprisingly much new evidence came out of this very limited operation (see St Cross chapter), and one of the broken gravestones recovered was that of Henry Antrobus.

Henry Antrobus was born and died in Knutsford; his dates are 1643-1716 and he was the proprietor of a drapery business in the town. The fact that both his father and one of his uncles were also named Henry Antrobus, and so was his grandfather, and that there was another draper's shop in town belonging to

Peter Antrobus, makes it prudent not to delve too deeply into Antrobusology.

They were a very extensive and numerous Cheshire family who were almost all mercers, shop-keepers, drapers, haberdashers. Among the preserved tradesmen's bills of Tabley House are the accounts with Henry Antrobus, draper, including quite large sums for black mourning cloth. The Antrobuses also had strong links with the City of London, St Paul's, and the company of Merchant Taylors.

Our Henry Antrobus had two sisters, Elizabeth who married James Swinton, and Margaret who married Joseph Furness. Henry was unmarried and both his sisters were childless and outlived their respective husbands; so that between them there was a tidy fortune to be disposed of. Most was given for the benefit of the minister of St John's, the school master, and the poor. Henry left £800 for the benefit of the town's poor, which was invested in a farm in a village called Antrobus. Now must be the time to consider the origin of that curious name. It is suggested that it is Norman French, like Malpas meaning bad way. Entre-bois - between the woods.

Henry Antrobus is known to have built six houses in the town. One was the last house before the Tatton Gate, which was left by his sister Margaret on her death in 1718 to be used as a Vicarage; now the Old Vicarage. Next door was another, taller and plainer with some good plaster ceilings preserved inside. Opposite the George and Dragon was the one we call the Patisserie. Next to that, on its right and its left, are the others.

The Old Vicarage is still very pretty from the outside but has lost its interiors. The Patisserie is the other way round; its exterior has been extensively altered but the interior is complete. It turns out that the splendid stair continues right to the top of the house in undiminished style; four floors, three straight creaky flights with square newels, exactly as Alison Uttley describes at the Old Vicarage. The internal structure of the building is entirely timber-framed, with unusual cross-bracing. Brick is reserved for the outside wall and the chimney stacks, which are rounded rather than angled in section in both buildings.

The high quality of the staircase implies that it was meant to be seen, and the fact that it goes from top to bottom implies that the whole house was meant to be seen. The explanation may be that this was Henry Antrobus's draper's shop, that the upper floors were used as well as the ground floor. As for the basement flight, it is in reality only a semi-basement; because of the fall of the land the back is at ground level. This would have opened onto a garden, or even alternative business access. There is a good original studded door here, although it seems too thin for an exterior one.

From Alison Uttley's description of the Old Vicarage it sounds more domestic than the Patisserie. But it should be remembered that there were two Antrobus shops in town.

The house to the immediate right of the Patisserie shows the same decorative brickwork on its facade, but no visible original internal features. The one on the other side, though contemporary, bears a different stamp. Currently a cafe bar called Est Piccolino it has its original oak staircase like the Patisserie but it is of a different plan, rising only one floor and spiralling round a newel rather than running in straight flights; evidently a less satisfactory construction because it has sagged inwards. In this house lived for a while the irascible but kind-hearted Dr Peter Holland, Elizabeth Gaskell's uncle, and Edmund Sharpe's too - see the St Cross chapter. He is the supposed model for Dr Gibson in 'Wives and Daughters'. Peter Holland acted as physician to most of the local gentry as well as the townsfolk; the Stanleys of Alderley, the Leicesters of Tabley, the Egertons of Tatton and occasionally the Langford-Brookes of Mere were all numbered among his patients. He also attended the apprentices, really workhouse children, at Samuel Greg's Quarry Bank Mill - a very early example of an industrial health programme. In spite of the high respect in which he was held as a physician

the mortality among his own children was about average for the time - three of the seven children of his first marriage died in infancy.

The Hollands were a talented and enterprising family, and thanks to Elizabeth Gaskell still quite a celebrated one. Peter's brother Swinton was a London banker and Samuel was an early industrial entrepreneur, promoting slate quarries in Wales and a tramway system, forerunner of the famous Ffestiniog railway, to bring the slates down from the mountains to the coast. Perhaps Edmund Sharpe, who features largely in the St Cross chapter, had his uncle Samuel in mind when he set forth on his own railway career.
It is sad that the Holland's country house, Sandlebridge Farm, has been demolished. The big farmhouse and the country round about was remembered with such fondness by Elizabeth Gaskell:-

(12 May 1836)
'Fancy me sitting in an old-fashioned parlour, 'doors and windows opened wide', with casement windows opening into a sunny court all filled with flowers which scent the air with their fragrance - in the very depth of the country - 5 miles from the least approach to a town - the song of birds, the hum of insects the lowing of cattle the only sounds - and such pretty fields & woods all round .....'

The countryside is still pretty round about, especially when the May is in blossom, but I wonder what she would think of the vast car boot sales held every Sunday in the neighbouring fields.

The eldest of Peter Holland's children, born in the King Street house in 1788, was the celebrated and amiable Dr and later Sir Henry Holland, even more celebrated as a physician than his father, although the ever cattily perceptive Maria Josepha, Lady Stanley, attributed this more to his smooth talk than scientific ability:-

(7th Feb 1806)

'He aims at being a London physician, and, if information and good sense could ensure success, he would have a fair chance of rising in that line to great eminence; but I think ignorance and plenty of small talk and flattery are more likely to succeed.'

Before settling in London he travelled abroad:-

(c1813 Martha Sharpe to William Whittaker):

'Henry Holland is expected home in May; he has been wintering in Athens, and has had the offer of a very advantageous settlement in one of the Greek Islands, from the Ali Pascha, who promised him a large salary and 12 wives if he would be his physician; was not that a princely offer? I suppose it is cheap living there, but the Pascha could not have devised a better plan for frightening the doctor away.'

He was briefly back in England in 1814, when the assessment of another one of his numerous relations chimes in with that of Lady Stanley:-

1st April 1814 Thomas Satterthwaite to Wm Whittaker at Cambridge:

'I suppose you will know that H Holland is fixed in the metropolis. Not a doubt of his doing well. What he has already written has brought him completely into notice, and his manners are, as far as I can recollect, for he never once condescended to speak to me, mild and amiable.'

before being summoned to Germany to attend the Princess of Wales. This was the start of an exalted medical career as the trusted physician to royalty and prime ministers, who could number among his friends and acquaintances most of the scientific intelligentsia of the day.

The Booths Town-house?

The next group to merit our attention, nearly opposite the churchyard wall, is a row of three shops occupying a low white building running parallel with the road. Old photographs show that these were once thatched, and that there was a fourth section.

There is little to remark upon from outside. Shop windows, white-painted brickwork, level slate roofs. Inside the shops timber-framing is evident, but it is only upstairs that the reason for selecting this particular group becomes apparent. Above Technotype is a fine room with rustic moulded plasterwork over the purlins and braces and a splendid decorated ceiling. A fat oval of plaster leaves surrounds a design of what is called strapwork. This dates it to about 1630, around the time of Hardwick and Montacute. Next door, above the Cheshire, there is an even more spectacular ceiling, again with an oval of leaves and strapwork, but this time there is a quartet of the most delicious angel trumpeters at the corners. Their hands are big and their feet are small, they kick their legs up under their frilled skirts, and their cheeks puff out to sound their trumpets, which are doubled back like slide trombones, with a narrow bell.

The third shop, a gentleman's outfitters, is stripped down to the wattle and daub and is open right to the roof with no upper floor.

How can we interpret this? It must have been a building of considerable status and pretension. It is known that the Leghs of Booths Hall had a house hereabouts. A photograph exists of an overmantel carrying their arms which, it is thought, was in the fourth of the row, now unrecognisable. Let us examine the evidence of the building.

The framing looks to be very much of the same period as the plasterwork, say 1630. There are blocked doorways linking the different shops, which implies that they were once one house, but looking more closely they are not original to the fabric but have been cut through at some subsequent stage.

The ceiling design above Technotype is not central but is pushed to one end with a blank bit at the other end. This must represent a chimney, or judging by its size, a whopping smoke hood. These were framed in timber but always separate from the main structure. Now we know what to look for we can see the shadow of another one in the outfitters shop.

Lastly we look again at the ceiling plasterwork. The natural assumption is that the two rooms go together as part of the same job, which would imply again that this was once a single dwelling; but there are unexpected detail differences. The leaves of the oval lie flat in the angel trumpeter ceiling, but stand free in the other. The strapwork designs are quite different although its overall design is roughly the same. It could just as well be a case of rivalry between neighbours.

The evidence that it was the Leghs' town house is, then, inconclusive.

Brook Street Chapel

Facing the end of King Street, although it is now impossible to cross over to for much of the day; on a grassy bank and framed by old trees, is the famous Nonconformist chapel of 1689. Famous not so much for itself, although it is a charming building in its homely simplicity, but because of its association with Elizabeth Gaskell. Here we meet the Antrobuses again. Henry Antrobus and his sisters supported the established church but Isaac their cousin would have none of it. Dissent was strong in Cheshire, often dividing families, and Knutsford was a major meeting place for the non-conforming Ministers. Isaac Antrobus gave part of his land -

he lived where The Grove was later to be built - for the chapel and was a principal contributor to its cost. He is buried beneath the centre aisle as is his son, also Isaac, who is commemorated in a quaint brass epitaph in Latin, for he was a schoolmaster.

Brook Street chapel was the first of a trio built to the same design although differing in flavour. The other two are in Macclesfield and at Dean Row. It is a neat design with matching outer staircases to the galleries at the two ends of the building. They were centrally planned, like the Calvinist churches of Holland, round a tall pulpit for the exposition of the word and a plain table for the Lord's supper. They are much more cottage-like than church-like, and very pleasing in their homely simplicity.

What are we to make of these buildings? The Heritage Centre building and the possible Booths town house show us the Cheshire vernacular tradition of building in oak. The blacksmith's is unaffected by any fashions or changes in the world at large, even though it may be of very late date, because it is a functional building. There was no reason to change building methods until the oak ran out or the fire risk became intolerable. The town house is essentially identical in its structure, but because it was a high-status building it is embellished with the latest thing in plasterwork.

The Antrobus houses and the chapel are particularly interesting because in them we can see the Renaissance hitting Knutsford.

Timelines, beloved of school historians, can be very misleading, assuming that time runs forward at the same rate all the time and in every place. We all know that this is not true, that it is possible to visit a place that is living in the past, or the future, simply by travelling. And yet certain ideas can cut across and short-circuit the differences in local time - the internet is a good example.

It is generally assumed that architectural styles follow an orderly timeline, but this is no more true than life in general. Here we have a group all dating from around 1700 and built by a single family.

In Italy the villas of Palladio were already 150 years old. Symmetry, restraint, proportion; Classicism made human, but not too human. In London the genial works of Christopher Wren were beginning to look a little old-fashioned - too robust, too English - as the influence of Palladio began to be felt. But in Rainow, just 15 miles from Knutsford up in the hills, the newly-builded Hall was purely medieval - no symmetry, latticed windows set between stone mullions; not a sign of the Renaissance. The heavy stone lintel over the off-centre door carries the date 1690. In Hale Barns there is a timber-framed barn entirely in the local vernacular tradition which is dated 1700.

Fashions take time to travel both geographically and down the social scale.

The Old Vicarage here is strictly symmetrical and it has brick pilasters, suggesting a hazy knowledge of Classical style.

The brickwork of the front is in the new Flemish bond, but untidily done. The windows, which are up-to-date sashes, are really too big for the building. Clearly a knowledge of the fashion, but falling down somewhat in the execution - which is why it is so charming.

The Patisserie is more old-fashioned, or less pretentious, with no attempt at classicising though it probably was symmetrical. Its structure shows exactly the moment when the old timber-framed tradition was overtaken by brick. The staircase is the thing here - very grand. The decorative leadwork hopper and downpipe on the front would have been quite a status symbol; and here we have an example of the differential rate of change because Rainow Hall has one as well. Perhaps the leadworker travelled further than the local mason.

Brook Street chapel although humbly domestic, with medieval style latticed and mullioned windows, is symmetrical although with no central emphasis - which is odd because on the inside the emphasis is all on the central pulpit. The symmetry is not an architectural conceit but an expression of its function - and yet surely this is as much an expression of the coming age and the rejection of all things gothic and medieval as the aesthetic preferences noted above. Like the other Antrobus buildings Brook Street chapel stands right on the dividing line of a new age. Forward looking in its symmetry and its central planning, backward in its rustic style, and in a curious feature that Raymond Richards noticed in his 'Old Cheshire Churches' of 1947, its alignment east-west, which is as medieval and superstitious as can be.

Brook St Chapel

Unit Chapel schools entrance.
Far right: Brook Street memorial to Rev H Green, author of 'Knutsford; its traditions and history'.

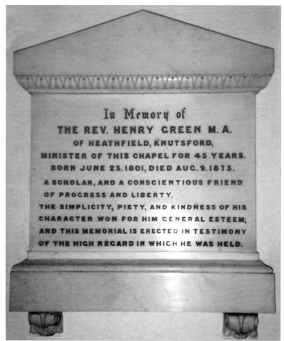

In Memory of
THE REV. HENRY GREEN M.A.
OF HEATHFIELD, KNUTSFORD,
MINISTER OF THIS CHAPEL FOR 45 YEARS.
BORN JUNE 23.1801, DIED AUG. 9.1873.
A SCHOLAR, AND A CONSCIENTIOUS FRIEND
OF PROGRESS AND LIBERTY.
THE SIMPLICITY, PIETY, AND KINDNESS OF HIS
CHARACTER WON FOR HIM GENERAL ESTEEM;
AND THIS MEMORIAL IS ERECTED IN TESTIMONY
OF THE HIGH REGARD IN WHICH HE WAS HELD.

Fragment of Henry
Antrobus's gravestone
from St Helena's

Knutsford signal box stood at the
top of the King Street bridge but wa
destroyed whilst this book was in
preparation.

Angel Trumpeters disport themselves above the Cheshire Building Society office! Was this part of a town house belonging to the Leghs of Booths Hall?

The Gaskell Tower when newly built.
This postcard also shows the Cross Keys in its original state
before rebuilding took place.

This engaging house carries the initials and date
H
J M
1721

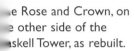

…e Rose and Crown, on
…e other side of the
…skell Tower, as rebuilt.

…: the Tatton end of King
…reet is this fine line-up of
…o Antrobus houses
…700 and the Ruskin
…ooms of 1902.

The Patisserie, built by Henry Antrobus in 1697 (see pages 36 and 42).

The Patisserie staircase

...11 and Tatton Park
...ckons invitingly beyond
...e Knutsford Gate. No
...tices or ticket offices
...en to spoil the effect -
...ntrast the picture
...erleaf.

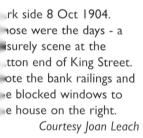

...rk side 8 Oct 1904.
...ose were the days - a
...isurely scene at the
...tton end of King Street.
...ote the bank railings and
...e blocked windows to
...e house on the right.

Courtesy Joan Leach

May Day sanding in the
Heritage Centre Yard.

May Day Parade 2000, setting off from Egerton School yard. Lady Stanley's sedan chair gets its annual outing.

The Knutsford Gate to Tatton Park in its present cluttered guise. Contrast the picture on the previous page.

Gorgeous Procession

Escorting the "Royal" May Queen,

By upwards of 400 Characters in NEW and COSTLY DRESSES, including NAVAL BRIGADE and CYCLISTS in Fancy Costumes.

CHARMING PERFORMANCES in the Enclosure on the Heath, including the Coronation of May Queen, etc. New and Fancy Dances, Plaiting the May Pole, Infants' Drill, and Morris Dancing as Danced in 'ye Olden Time.

Admission to Stand, 1/-; Covered Stand, 2/6; Carriages, 2/6 & 5/-; Waggonettes & Omnibuses, 15/-; Ring Enclosure, 6d.

Dancing will commence immediately the Children have left the Ring.

ADMISSION TO DANCE RING, 3d.

"Let me bid you welcome."

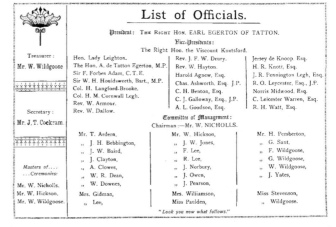

List of Officials.

President: THE RIGHT HON. EARL EGERTON OF TATTON.

Vice-Presidents:

The Right Hon. the Viscount Knutsford.

Treasurer: Mr. W. Wildgoose

Secretary: Mr. J. T. Cockram.

Hon. Lady Leighton.
The Hon. A. de Tatton Egerton, M.P.
Sir F. Forbes Adam, C.T.E.
Sir W. H. Houldsworth, Bart., M.P.
Col. H. Langford-Brooke.
Col. H. M. Cornwall Legh.
Rev. W. Armour.
Rev. W. Dallow.

Rev. J. F. W. Drury.
Rev. W. Hayton.
Harold Agnew, Esq.
Chas. Ashworth, Esq. J.P.
C. H. Benton, Esq.
C. J. Galloway, Esq., J.P.
A. L. Goodson, Esq.

Jersey de Knoop, Esq.
H. R. Knott, Esq.
J. R. Pennington Legh, Esq.
R. O. Leycester, Esq., J.P.
Norris Midwood, Esq.
C. Leicester Warren, Esq.
R. H. Watt, Esq.

Committee of Management:

Chairman:—Mr. W. NICHOLLS.

Masters of....
...Ceremonies:
Mr. W. Nicholls.
Mr. W. Hickson.
Mr. W. Wildgoose.

Mr. T. Ardern,
„ J. H. Bebbington,
„ J. W. Baird,
„ J. Clayton,
„ A. Clowes,
„ W. R. Dean,
„ W. Downes,
Mrs. Gidman,
„ Lee,

Mr. W. Hickson,
„ J. W. Jones,
„ F. Lee,
„ R. Lee,
„ J. Norbury,
„ J. Owen,
„ J. Pearson,
Mrs. Williamson,
Miss Paulden,

Mr. H. Pemberton,
„ G. Sant,
„ F. Wildgoose,
„ G. Wildgoose,
„ W. Wildgoose,
„ J. Yates,

Miss Stevenson,
„ Wildgoose.

"Look you now what follows."

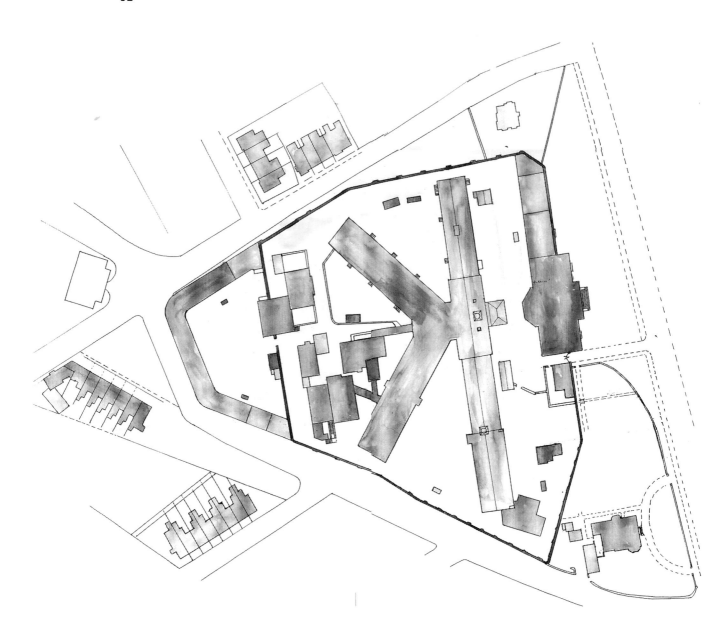

Three
THE SESSIONS HOUSE AND GOAL

The County Sessions - the building of the sessions house and gaol 1818 - Harrison or Moneypenny? - biographical details. The gaol - dead land? - life in the goal - closure - conscientious objectors 1914-18 - the Test School 1919 and its origin in Flanders - demolition of the gaol. Booth's supermarket.

The Sessions House

'Duly grave' says Pevsner (Buildings of England - Cheshire 1971), neatly characterising the Sessions House in just two words.

There is a language of the law: gravity, probity, strength, permanence. Hence the solemn portico, the great size and weight of the stones, the powerful symmetry, the huge keystones hanging poised over the entrances, the smooth perfection of the ashlar. Everything tells of the Majesty of the Law and the smallness of those who are caught up in its machinations, from which there is no escape for the guilty. There are no windows.

To one side stands the house of the governor of the gaol, now town council offices, and to the other the police. Behind was the gaol itself, four storeys high and grim as grim, looming over a twenty-foot wall. The mighty portico of the Sessions House acted as focus and frontispiece for all this.

In the year 1737 the market hall and sessions chamber at Nantwich, then the second town of Cheshire, fell down; which calamity was attended with considerable loss of life. It would have been a timber-framed structure on legs, like the one which can still be seen at Leominster. The old Leominster sessions house carries inscriptions suitable to its purpose:-
LIKE AS COLLVMNS DOO VPPROP THE FABRIK OF A BVILDING SO NOBLE GENTRY DOO SUPPORT THE HONOR OF A KINGDOM, and WHERE JUSTICE RVLE: THERE VIRTV FLOW.

The twice-yearly County Sessions were transferred from Nantwich to Knutsford. Being largely conducted by members of the neighbouring noble gentry they were the occasions of considerable social gaiety in the town. The first Sessions House was at the end of Princess Street or Top Street opposite the Heath, to be replaced by the present 'duly grave' edifice in 1818.

Who was the architect? The credit has in the past generally gone to Thomas Harrison of Chester and Lancaster, but more recently George Moneypenny has gained the honours; it is his name that appears on the explanatory plaque under the portico.

Personally I go for both of them. My own opinion is that the carcass of the Sessions House is by Harrison, but that the execution of it was probably in the hands of Moneypenny, who also designed the interiors and the pepperpot turret perched over the portico. I think that Moneypenny probably designed and executed the goal in consultation with Harrison.

Thomas Harrison (1744-1829) was the leading neoclassical architect of the day, certainly in the north of England. We know quite a lot about him. On Sunday December 20th 1795, after church, Joseph Farington, Royal Academician, topographical artist, and gossip (if that word does not imply too frivolous a character), dined at Mr Baker's in London; Hearne, Marchant and Harrison were there. This is what he recorded in his diary :-

'Harrison has been employed at Lancaster in building some additions to the castle for the reception of felons. In these additions he has not used any wood; the whole being formed of stone & iron occasionally used. The roofs of the upper apartments are composed of stone only, and the manner of they are laid is composed thus:

[a diagram follows, showing stones laid corbel-wise]

Harrison is a plain man in person & manners, with an embarrassed delivery in conversation, but very clear and ready in explaining with his pencil. He was born at Richmond in Yorkshire. His father was a carpenter. When a young man his talents were so conspicuous, that Sir Thomas Dundass was induced to send him to Italy, where he remained 6 or 7 years.'

Farington's thumbnail sketch has stood as Harrison's general epitaph these two centuries.

Harrison's works at Lancaster Castle are highly impressive, showing a talent for geometry and a great feeling for the strength and stoniness of that mighty stronghold. However he left the new works at Lancaster incomplete when he received a commission to carry out a similar but more ambitious project at Chester Castle, which was to occupy him for the rest of his long life. It was characteristic of him to lose interest once the structural work was done - he had little interest in decoration and fitting out.

Chester Castle is a great achievement, a picturesque classical composition on the grandest scale. A powerful Doric portico frowns over a great open parade ground, flanked by a matching pair of Ionic palaces, and approached through a three-part propylea. It all seems too spread out today and it is very hard to enjoy the spatial relationships between the different parts. This is because we have cluttered the whole place up. The great parade ground should be animated by marching and countermarching soldiers, preferably in scarlet and led by a band - not full of dead metal in the shape of parked cars.

Let CR Cockerell, aesthete, scholar and classical architect, take up the story. He visited Harrison in his new house, St Martin's Lodge, in 1823 and noted in his diary :-

'Harrison is undoubtedly the noblest genius in arche. we have in external arche. chiefly. He has a secret exultation in his fine works & his merits, but mixed with great truth and modesty.

Walked over Chester Castle with great pleasure. Certainly a great hand is visible. It is open to criticism in many points, most obviously in the variety of Doric orders in the propylea & court & in the Ionic sides, each seemingly by a different hand, but it is in the great intelligence of the masonry that Harrison's merit lies.'

A shrewd assessment. It is indeed worth studying the masonry, for both Cockerell and Harrison knew that it is in the great size and weight of the stones together with the perfection of their working that the true virtue of grand classical architecture lies; this is the quality that distinguishes the Knutsford Sessions House.

Cockerell goes on to note :- 'At Chester six monoliths of ten tons each were placed on their pedestals one night before the Court of Justice. The effect next day on the magistrates was so great that they allowed him to carry out certain matters in which his taste and judgment might otherwise have been over-ruled.'

As well they might indeed. It is a wonder how these great stones were transported and handled. At Chester they would need only to be dragged a short distance from the Dee, although it is a considerable climb. The nearest point to Knutsford for water transport must I suppose have been the Weaver at Northwich. What a job that must have been!

Before we leave Harrison we must note that he bears some responsibility for one of the great cultural controversies of the present time, one which is not going to go away until it is resolved. I refer to the Elgin Marbles.

It was Harrison who first suggested to Lord Elgin that he make a study of the ancient Greek architecture of Athens. Elgin, for whom Harrison had designed his Scottish mansion, had just been appointed ambassador in Constantinople, and Greece was then a Turkish dependency. As part of the proposed study drawings and plaster casts were to be made, but as yet there was no suggestion of actually taking anything away from the ruins. Elgin was enthusiastic, and on travelling out to his embassy set a team of artists, measurers and moulders to work on the buildings of the Acropolis. How this work turned into the removal of chunks of sculpture is currently sub judice so to speak.

Byron was there. Initially he took a took a jaundiced view of Lord Elgin's efforts:-
... Let Aberdeen and Elgin still pursue
The shades of fame through regions of virtu;
Waste useless thousands on their Phidian freaks,
Misshapen monuments and maim'd antiques;
And make their grand saloons an general mart
For all the mutilated blocks of art.
[English Bards and Scotch Reviewers 1809]

Later, having seen the results of the despoilation, and Elgin's name carved on what was left, he waxed furious. Here he imagines Pallas Athene herself speaking to him from the ruins:-

'"Mortal!" 'twas thus she spake -
"that blush of shame
Proclaims thee Briton, once a noble name;
First of the mighty, foremost of the free,
Now honour'd less by all, and least by me:
Chief of thy foes shall Pallas still be found.
Seeks't thou the cause of loathing? - look around.
Lo! here, despite of war and wasting fire,
I saw successive tyrannies expire.
'Scaped from the ravage of the Turk and Goth,
Thy country sends a spoiler worse than both.
Survey this vacant, violated fane;
Recount the relics torn that yet remain:

.....

That all may learn from whence the plunderer
came,
The insulted wall sustains his hated name:
For Elgin's fame thus grateful Pallas pleads,
Below his name - above, behold his deeds!
Be ever hail'd with equal honour here
The Gothic monarch and the Pictish peer:
Arms gave the first his right, the last had none
But basely stole what less barbarian won.
So when the lion quits his fell repast,
Next prowls the wolf, the filthy jackal last:
Flesh, limbs, and blood the former make his own,
The last poor brute securely gnaws the bone.'

This is from 'The Curse of Minerva', written in Athens, at the Capuchin Convent March 17th 1811. It was the age of scurrilous cartoons and waspish verse, but perhaps only a fellow peer would have dared call Lord Elgin a filthy jackal.

We will let Charles Cockerell have the last word :-

'As we were sailing out of the port in our open boat we overtook the ship with Lord Byron on board. Passing under her stern we sang a favourite song of his, on which he looked out of the windows and invited us in. There we drank a glass of port with him ...'

Cockerell was on his way over to Aegina from the Piraeus, Athens, on the 22nd April 1811. The ship was the Hydra and was carrying not just Lord Byron but the last consignment of the Elgin Marbles back to England. When they got to England and were finally uncrated they caused an artistic sensation, powerfully fuelling the move towards Grecian purity in architecture which was to produce the Knutsford Sessions House, even if Knutsford couldn't afford any sculptural decoration for it.

I cannot resist adding a postscript, for international controversies sometimes have the most unexpected local repercussions. Regular visitors to the Manchester Museum often ask "what has happened to the Iguanadon?". The said Iguanadon, a most impressive fossilised dinosaur, was on loan to Manchester from the British Museum. It is now in Athens, having been sent there by the British Museum as a peace offering. I fear it cannot be enough.

So Mr Harrison was I think at the very least the guiding spirit for the new Sessions House. As surveyor to the County of Chester it is most unlikely he not have been involved, and moreover the quality of the stonework points to him; indeed the fine orange sandstone employed here appears to be the same as the one he used at Chester Castle and at the Portico Library in Manchester.

George Moneypenny on the other hand made a speciality of building gaols, at a time when this was a lucrative line to be in. His dates are 1768-1830 so he was a good deal younger than Harrison. His father, also George Moneypenny, was a stonemason and sculptor, one of a circle of contractors, artisans and artists who gained a living at the feet of the local aristocracy. Joseph Pickford the architect and contractor, Joseph Wright of Derby the painter, Samuel Wyatt the agent and architect-to-be, Samuel Renn the organ builder, not to mention a host of skilled craftsmen, all of these would have known each other and have found employment at a major site like Kedleston working under the exalted and gentlemanly Robert Adam.

Apart from the gaol the interior finishing and decoration of the two courts is probably the work of Mr Moneypenny. The large court is a very grand chamber although it has been cut about by modern partitioning. It is curious to note that the end wall behind the judge's seat is a gentle curve; on the outside it is angled. Although considerably more grand, it is very like the Court of Law at Ruthin, designed by Joseph Turner, which has been very successfully converted into the town library.

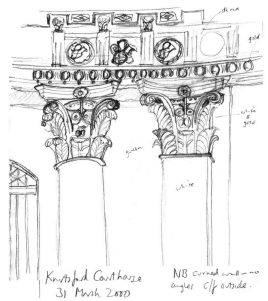

Knutsford Courthouse
31 March 2000

NB curved wall — no angles c/f outside.

Architects are often criticised for not living in their own buildings, and therefore not being aware of their faults. This criticism cannot be levelled at Mr Moneypenny. At Leicester, where he was contractor as well as architect for the new county gaol, he got into financial difficulties and was consequently locked up for some time in his own gaol. It would be nice to know if he made any design improvements in consequence.

The Gaol

It is hard to imagine today the effect on the smiling town of Knutsford of a huge and grim goal bang in the middle of it. Yet it was there in

Elizabeth Gaskell's day, just a few yards from her childhood home, and it was there, though no longer housing felons, until the mid 1930s. Why was it built here? Working on the 'nimby' principle, prisons and places of execution are often built on land which is not in anybody's back yard; on boundaries and in between major landholdings. Could this apply to the Knutsford site? A clue is given by the big rough boulder which pokes through the tarmac on the side street called Church View, by the little classical Savings Bank on Princess Street. It looks like an ancient boundary stone or mere stone, although there is no way of dating a thing like this. That stone marks a line that goes clean through the town from Bexton Road, along one side of the gaol site, and then down the alley to the Moor. For this theory to hold water one would hope to find other markers at the other two apices of the triangle, somewhere near the railway bridge and by the Bucklow Union office.

Many prisons were built at this period. The concept of imprisoning someone for a civil offence was a relatively new one. In older times punishments ranged from the stocks to hanging, with transportation being a more recent alternative.

What was the old gaol like? If you would know, take a trip to Beaumaris on Anglesey, where the little prison of 1829 is open for viewing by the public. It is a salutary experience. Not as unmitigatedly grim as one might expect, for it is well-organised and much

thought has gone into tempering the punishment with a degree of humanity. Its small size renders it surprisingly engaging, but of course now all the doors are open, the keys are thrown away, and we are free to leave when we please. Some things still strike cold; especially the treadmill, which was designed to use up prisoners' energy. Not the big open wheel of medieval building sites, but an enclosed machine with a row of narrow slots up which eight or ten prisoners in a line trudged for an hour at a time, with a B team waiting to take over. Pause or break the rhythm and the wheel will break your leg. Here, as at Knutsford, the treadmill pumped water up into big square tanks on top of the roofs, looking like outsize chimneys.

The whole thing was designed for easy surveillance, so the wings radiated out from a central observation point, like a T at Beaumaris but a giant K at Knutsford. At Beaumaris the central corridors are floored with great slabs of slate but generally, as at Knutsford, all floors were made simultaneously visible by making great long atria lit from above, and accessing the levels of cells from flying galleries of iron.

As there is a language of the law so even more so there is a language of prisons. It is not enough that escape is impossible - the gaol must cow your spirit and discourage you from even thinking of escape. It is no accident that the cell door bangs shut behind you, the sound reverberating through the stony galleries of the gaol. It says what needs to be said. The bars are always much thicker than is strictly necessary, the window smaller and higher, the floor colder and the walls sweatier.

The Test School

Knutsford Goal became redundant in the early years of the 20th century due to a falling prison population. It was empty at the outset of the First World War.

The Great War was an extraordinary and appalling episode in European history, still gripping to the imagination. So many young men, such boyish high hopes, enduring such unimaginable squalor and brought face to face with such ghastly death. It is hard to remember how young they all were. The whole futile calamity is summarised for me in this little extract from a letter written by Ivor Gurney somewhere on the western front on July 16th 1916:-

'The machine gunners manage to make their job more interesting by "playing tunes" on their guns. As thus. After the ordinary casual shots and steady pour, one hears

which always sounds comic, and must, I imagine require some skill."

Ivor Gurney, like most men, went willingly enough to the slaughter; but those few brave or awkward souls who refused to fight, the 'conchies' or conscientious objectors, were considered dangerous enough to the morale of the country to need to be locked up. Soon too there were prisoners-of-war. So the old goal at Knutsford came into use again.

After the armistice at the end of the Great War came its final brief role. It was an astonishing episode of history in which Knutsford came to play a unique part.

The story started in the mud of Flanders, in the Ypres salient. This is a ring of low hills which surrounds the ancient city of Ypres, or 'Wipers' - Ieper today. Any sort of eminence or vantage point in this flat landscape was strategically valuable, and the salient was attacked over and over again for the whole of the four years with dreadful loss of life and hideous devastation; but it held - the only part of Belgium to do so. Ypres was destroyed bit by bit by pitiless shells, until all that was left of the town, the Flemish crow-stepped houses, the famous medieval cloth hall and the cathedral of St Martin, was a few piles of rubble with roadways cleared between them. Although successfully defended, life here was pretty well insupportable. Running back from Ypres towards the coast was a straight narrow road raised a few feet above the flat farmland and a single track railway line. This was the supply line. All the troops had to pass this way in ceaseless movement, all the artillery, supplies, ammunition; and back the other way came the wounded and the exhausted. The road and the railway passed through the battered village of Vlamertinge and then about ten kilometres back from Ypres the little town of Poperinge. This nondescript town took on a peculiar importance to the thousands of Allied soldiers who passed this way because it was the last place where any sort of normal life was possible.

Here on the main street, in a tall old white house, a merchant's house with a big hop-loft, an Army chaplain established a home-from-home for the war-weary, a refuge from the horrific scenes and the constant threat of death or mutilation which was every soldier's lot.

'*Here there is a <u>garden</u>. There are <u>trees</u>. the <u>birds</u> are <u>singing</u>.*' wrote a soldier on the regulation postcard home.

The house was called Talbot House. The unassuming chaplain who was its heart and soul called himself the Innkeeper or PBC - Philip Clayton, always called 'Tubby'.

Talbot House and PBC came to mean more to more people than we, who have not been through what they did, can possibly imagine. The old house had a special atmosphere about it. Indeed it still does for it is still there and you can still stay there. It is one of the holy places, but without making any effort about it, for the atmosphere was always hearty and noisy and full of good humour. PBC made the hop-loft above the house, only accessible up a steep ladder, into a chapel, intensely moving in its simplicity and silence, shedding its benign influence unseen on the busy house below. Up here thousands of soldiers made their first, their last, their most intense communion with God.

Tubby Clayton gradually came to see that something good, something precious, was coming into being right here under his roof, engendered by the terrible war and encouraged by the egalitarian spirit of the house. 'ALL RANK ABANDON YE WHO ENTER HERE' was one of the characteristic notices that were scattered about the corridors, among such frivolous ones as 'DOWN THESE STAIRS IN SIGNAL PHIAL'. He also realised that, as the country's young men were being wiped out in front of his eyes, so the church after the war would find itself desperately short of candidates for the priesthood. So he began to take down names of any young men who thought they might, in peacetime, consider ordination. He wrote them on pieces of card, and he put them in a tin trunk.

By the end of the war that tin trunk contained many hundreds of names. Many of the young men who had left them there were dead; many would change their minds, but many were steadfast. What would or could the church do about it, in the dark days after the war? Something had to be done immediately, or never, for the soldiers were being demobbed and soon the chance would be lost. The church had never taken on a large scale training before, where vocations could be nurtured and tested. Who would teach them? Where could instant accommodation be found for upwards of five hundred men? There simply was no such place available, unless .... he would consider an empty lunatic asylum or a gaol. Tubby characteristically retorted that the asylums should be reserved for General Staff. He opted for a goal.

And so it was that, in January 1919, two young men huddled in greatcoats got off the last train onto the snowy platform of Knutsford station. Let him continue the tale:-

'The time was not far short of midnight when we found a policeman and asked our way to the prison. "Prison?" he said, focussing his lantern upon us; "you'll find that soon enough if you're not careful." Assuring him of our good faith, we thought it best to ask for another destination for the night, and enquired for any hostelry which would have us in. His reply, so far as I remember, was that there were two: the "Angel" kept by Mr George, and the "George", kept by Mr Angell.

Knutsford, as it stood revealed the following morning, fascinated us completely ..... We made our way to the prison, and found it for the most part occupied by conscientious objectors, of whom we were told that a few were frauds and a few sheer saints. The place fascinated us from the first, and then and there, provided the authorities on both sides confirmed our judgment, we found the goal of our endeavours.

The elephantine humour of its long-forgotten and forgiven architect had built this stupendous nightmare in the form of a "K", each arm of which contained upon four floors about two hundred cells....'

(the quotes are from 'Plain Tales from Flanders' by Rev PB Clayton)

The first students arrived on 26 March 1919. Their first task was to make the dreadful old place habitable and give it some cheer.

'The execution-house was locked, but to men who had seen what these men had witnessed there was no morbid curiosity in such directions. Only one Greatheart, so desperately wounded that no game he loved would ever find him on the field of play again, devoted every afternoon, month after month, to making, with much toil, a lovely little garden above the ill-omened and unsightly place of burial, marked only on the inner wall by a series of initials and dates.'

A second batch arrived on the 17th of May and the school settled into a makeshift routine. Meals were cooked by a contingent of WAAFs in the prison kitchens and eaten at long rows of trestle tables in the corridors. Lectures were held in the Sessions House and in army huts put up in the exercise yards (Is there one left at the old Egerton School?). Games were on the Heath and there was fresh air in the Cheshire countryside.

'.... spring swept forward, so radiant in its coming to these men that they could scarcely credit it for joy. Year after year the coming of spring in Flanders had meant the lifting of an ominous curtain which hung before another awful period of wounds and death and all but unendurable affliction; there had not been a man upon that whole battle-line who did not know within his heart that either he or those beside him would never see the new green leaves turn brown. Now we were free, as men delivered from a furnace, to come and go about the lanes of Cheshire and test the rights of way, whose use establishes the common liberties if the people.'

The whole Test School episode only lasted three or four years, filling the grim old prison for the first and only time of its entire existence with hope and joy. An astonishing photograph in St John's church, which they used in preference to the gloomy prison chapel, testifies to the impact several hundred idealistic young men must have had on the town. It is estimated that 675 candidates were trained in all, of whom 435 were eventually ordained.

Its job done, a much diminished Test School moved first to Kilrie, an ugly Victorian mansion on the Tabley Road which is under threat of demolition at the time of writing, then In 1922 to Hawarden.

'The whole adventure of Knutsford seems incredible. It was, by any count, sheer audacity to take several hundred men of different educational and social backgrounds, lump them together in a disused prison, and then proceed to prepare them for the great universities and theological colleges. But any of those men .... would have been totally lost to the Church if the Innkeeper of Talbot House had been respectful of tradition or intimidated by obstacles. Tubby had always been scornful of the "gentleman tradition" which drew its clergy only from a sealed privileged section of society. .. There were but two qualifications - character and education, and the education, wherever necessary, should be provided by the church.' (This is from 'Tubby Clayton - a personal saga' by Melville Harcourt 1956)

All the time that the Test School was operating in Knutsford Tubby Clayton had another and even bigger scheme in mind. He wished to recreate the fellowship of Talbot House in England, and to take it forward into peacetime. All he had was a large bag full of signed slips of paper, several thousand of them, each one bearing the name of a communicant at the Old House in Pop. The publication of his little book 'Tales of Talbot House' in September 1919 served as the first rallying call. On the night of 14th November he went down to London from Knutsford for an initial meeting to consider his idea. The agenda was written in mock-military style, its jocularity as usual with him covering a serious purpose:-

'the attack on the problem of re-opening Talbot House will be carried out by a Round Table Conference thirty in number, troops being drawn from Talbotousians past, present, and to come. The attack will be covered by a creeping barrage of business advisers, supported by expert Londoners. A section of Clerical Tanks will co-operate.

The vital need of maintaining the old fellowship and extending it to the younger clerks, civil servants and students of London offers special opportunity for initiative of all arms, and risks must be boldly taken.'

What emerged from this historic meeting and was to grow into a huge world-wide fellowship, was Toc H. Toc H is First World War signalling slang for Talbot House. Now it would be Tango Hotel.

The two great outcomes of the First World War which derived from Talbot House in the Ypres Salient were the Knutsford Test School and Toc H. In that order.

Booth's

Following the departure of the Test School the old gaol at Knutsford stood empty again. A wall was built across the site behind the Sessions House and it was unceremoniously demolished, bringing to a close a hundred years of degradation and misery and three of hope and joy. A small park was created on the site, with tennis courts, called Stanley Park, with a bus station on the Bexton Road side.

In 1978 the site was earmarked for a new library; this is a project which in the year 2000 has still to come to fruition - see the library chapter. Instead a competition was held by Macclesfield Borough Council to develop the site for a supermarket, which was won by Booth's and Co of Preston. The winning design was by Gill Dockray and Partners of Kendal; the project architect was John Davies.

Working within quite a tightly constrained site the architect has produced a very successful building in my opinion. It is oriented on the Sessions House, in fact the centre line from the Sessions House determines the whole design of both the supermarket and the landscaping. The supermarket with its three-sided 'open arms' entrance reflects and complements the three-sided apse of the large court overlooking the carpark. The centre walkway of the carpark links the two, and the small public park at the back - actually the least successful element - links this axis with that of the Bucklow Union building. Thus the new building is securely anchored into the fabric of Knutsford. A '60s architect would have pointedly ignored it all.

In the closing decades of the 20th century there seem to have been two architectural influences which it was very hard to escape, whether you were building a new church or a museum or indeed a leisure complex or supermarket, namely Tesco's and Disney. Tesco style is the large shed disguised by a fake pitched roof and corner turrets with weathervanes. Disney is the tendency to cheap caricature which bugs all attempts at imitating historical style - like the (very) mock-Georgian offices on Tatton Street. Here it seems to me that the architects have managed to avoid both dread influences. There is nothing mock-historical about it but it is not a decorated shed either. The pitched roof is a pitched roof, not just a gesture to the local civic society. The complex structure is clearly visible inside, indeed it is made a feature of, the white-painted tubular steelwork exhibiting strength but not crudity. Some daylight is admitted, which is bonus.

I am told that this, Booth's 21st store, is their most successful in its annual turnover. With its town centre location it seems to strengthen the town rather than fatally weakening it as most such superstores do.

There are two Anglican churches in Knutsford. Neither is particularly old, which is surprising

Harrison - or is it Moneypenny? - in Greek mode in Knutsford.

Thomas Harrison in Gothic mode at Lancaste Castle

Knutsford Gaol, now Booth's Car park, with a glimpse of the courthouse to right. Note the attempts at gardening which date this photograph to the Test School years.
Courtesy Cheshire County Council

The exercise yards, with concentric paths far enough apart to prevent prisoners from talking to each other.
Courtesy Joan Leach

Knutsford Gaol
Courtesy Joan Lea

One of the cells, looking
each way.
Courtesy Joan Lea

Warder's Houses. still
around the site of the
gaol.

Sessions House rear view,
facing Booth's car park.
Note the three-sided
courtroom which appears
in the gaol photograph on
the previous page.

THE LANGUAGE OF THE LAW

Ruthin Courthouse by Joseph Turner 1776. Now the town's library.

Knutsford Sessions House by Harrison or Moneypenny 1818.

Nottingham County Court
Joseph Gandon.
*Illustrated in Vitrunis
Britannicus*

Chester Crown
Court by Thomas
Harrison

OUR COAT OF ARMS

The imaginative blazoning of our Coat of Arms should not be taken seriously, or it will lead to court marshall at the College of Heralds. We flatter ourselves that no County Family, however ancient, nor any riche however nouveau, has used the space to such advantage. Men and brethren, the shield is quarterly.

(1) You will observe A Barry of six Nebuly Azure and Gules. A Pole-axe Argent, Helved Or. The Barry should be "in Chief" but this we have had to forego. [Rev. F B Barry, DSO, was Principal of the Test School]. The pole-axe has no hidden meaning that we have yet invented, but (1) reminds us that bully-beef is a thing of the past, and (2) relates pleasantly to the bull's head caboshed on the ground floor.

(2) Vert, on a Chevron Or between three Keys Or, three Broad Arrows Sable; on a Base a Rainbow proper. The keys lying about on the grass indicate what will happen to our neighbour's portable groan-box, if he persists in playing it in prep time.

(3) Azure, a Portcullis Or, surmounted by a Mitre of the last. This recalls to us the nature of our habitation, together with the intriguing legend of the Iron Gates of Alderley Edge.

(4) Or, a Bull's Head Caboshed Proper. This is the coat of the Sykes family, granted by William the Conqueror to the Grandfather. Why it is in the ground floor window on the right hand side every schoolboy knows.
[Rev F H Sykes OBE was Vice-Principal of the Test School]

This was the cover of the first edition of the Test School magazine in 1919. *"Ran into a meeting of the Magazine Committee. I shall certainly not buy a copy, for I hear they are going to call it "Ducdame", a Greek invocation for calling fools into a circle. The very idea!"* (c/f Jacques in 'As You Like It').

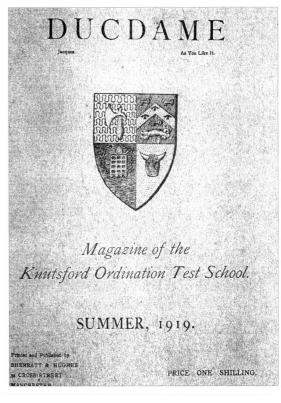

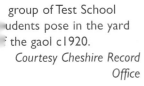

A group of Test School students pose in the yard of the gaol c1920.
Courtesy Cheshire Record Office

The Chief

Pictures from the Test School years at Knutsford Gaol
(see page 59)

aol Kitchen Staff
*Courtesy Cheshire County
Council*

udents breakfasting in
e long corridors of the
ol.
*Courtesy Cheshire County
Council*

Test School Students ma[ke]
the best of one of the ol[d]
cells

*Courtesy Cheshire Coun[ty]
Coun[cil]*

Students outside their ce[ll]
*Courtesy Cheshire Coun[ty]
Coun[cil]*

lbot House at
peringe, Flanders, or
c H for short, is where
e Knutsford Test School
iginated. The modern
ilding in front is where,
Tubby Clayton's words,
*shell knocked the
ighbouring house into
cocked hat'.*

r left: Ladder to upper
apel, Poperinge

lbot House chapel
peringe.

lbot House at Poperinge
Flanders. The Test
hool at Knutsford Gaol
d its origins here in the
ears of the First World
Var, see page 59.

Far left: The Cloth Hall at Ypres, miraculously rebuilt after its near destruction in the First World War.
Left: Tubby Clayton's 'groan-box', which accompanied him to the trenches.

Garden at Talbot House. The notice says 'Come into the garden and forget about the War'.

This was Toc H Mark IV in Manchester, founded in 1922.
Tubby Clayton started a fashion for little dogs - one is still
remembered here.

Kilvie, on the Tabley Road, was the last home of the Test School in Knutsford before it moved to Hawarden.

Kilvie stables.

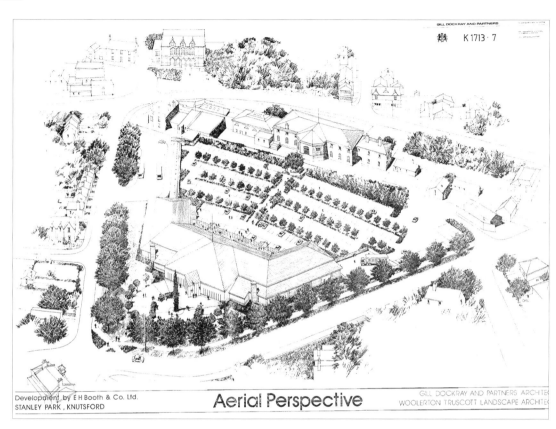

GILL DOCKRAY AND PARTNERS

K 1713 · 7

Development by E H Booth & Co. Ltd.
STANLEY PARK , KNUTSFORD

Aerial Perspective

GILL DOCKRAY AND PARTNERS ARCHITEC
WOOLERTON TRUSCOTT LANDSCAPE ARCHITEC

e Gaol site today -
oth's supermarket and
park.

Courtesy Booth's

Four
ST CROSS CHURCH

Churches in Knutsford - the ancient Rostherne parish - St Helena's parochial chapel - recent discoveries. The first St. Cross 1858. The second St Cross 1880 - Messrs Austin and Paley, architects - Edmund Sharpe of Knutsford, founder of the firm - his biography and family connections - Galloways and "biler 'all".

in so historic a town. Both are brick and square-towered, and they face each other across the open space and pool of the Moor.

The Lily, which runs along the roadway that edges the Moor, must be one of the smallest and shortest watercourses to attain the name River. It is only a few hundred yards long from its uprising in Mollypots or Sanctuary Moor to its fall into Tatton Mere, and it is almost everywhere narrow enough to step over; but it effectively cuts Knutsford in half. West of the Lily is today's town centre, formerly called Nether Knutsford, with its Georgian church of St John. On the other side is Crosstown or Higher Knutsford, and the Victorian St Cross.

Until St John's was built in 1744 Knutsford was just a part of the huge parish of Rostherne, so before that it never did have its own parish church. The ancient St Mary's, beautifully situated above the mysterious Rostherne Mere but now loud with motorways and planes, is way out to the north of Tatton Park. The church is clearly much too big for its diminutive village; the size of its graveyard is a good indication of the size of its original parish.

The ancient parishes in Cheshire and Lancashire are often enormous. Prestbury included no less than 32 townships, including Macclesfield, and the parish of Manchester was almost as big as its present Diocese. The reason lies in the dread words in Domesday:- 'vasta est' - it is laid waste. So when the parish system came into being the population hereabouts was greatly depleted and impoverished. As the region slowly gained prosperity after the depredations of the Norman invaders so chapelrys of one sort or another were built within the parishes. Serving Knutsford there was a Parochial Chapel dedicated to St Helena near Norbury Booths Hall, and a more convenient Chapel-of-Ease in the town in King Street; a plaque marks the spot.

St Helena's

Nothing of St Helena's remains visible today but its evocative site, a tree-ringed enclosure on a low hilltop near a stream, still surrounded by grassland, is somewhat municipalised today. It takes a bit of finding; from St Cross a beeline eastwards will lead by a series of footpaths and estate roads to the site - or not; it is easy to take a wrong turn and miss it.

A low ditch and bank encloses the old churchyard, within which a rectangle of 17th century grave slabs, handsomely lettered, marks the approximate position of the church itself. It was pretty small, and almost certainly timber-framed, with a stone tower that was added in the time of Henry VIII. The earliest written records of the church are of 1398 and 1476. However an archaeological watching brief carried out in March 2000 during Council work on the site turned up some surprises. A number of broken gravestones were found, including that of Henry Antrobus and Margaret his sister who feature in the King Street chapter. Among the stones were two or three fragments of something quite different; dark red and soft when compared with the hard grey 17th century gravestones; they are incised with a cross design standing on a stepped base. These few broken stones put the date of St Helena's back two hundred years, for they indicate a date of around 1200. It therefore antedates the charter of the town, so it is not so surprising that it is apparently so inconveniently situated. It is interesting to read (St Cross papers) that in 1873 a broken slab of a similar dark red stone was found buried face-down, which on raising was discovered to have three crosses cut into it, one in the centre and two in the corners. It was assumed that this was the ancient altar stone, which would have

had five crosses when whole. Such stone altars were outlawed at the Reformation, as pertaining more to a sacrifice than a shared meal at a table.

The dedication to St Helen is interesting, especially in a place sometimes called

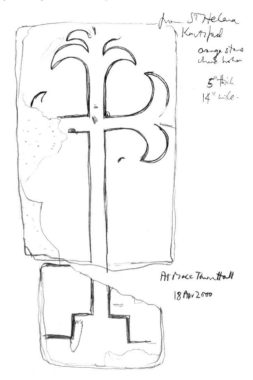

Crosstown and where the eventual successor church was dedicated to St Cross. Helen was the finder of the true cross. She was the wife or concubine of a Roman general called Constantius Chlorus, and in about 274 bore him a son called Constantine. In the year 306 Constantine was proclaimed Emperor at York: a fact honoured by a the new statue outside the south transept of the Minster.

The Roman empire was divided.

Constantine conquered his rivals, famously seeing a vision of a flaming cross before the battle of the Milvian bridge, bearing the legend 'In this sign conquer'. He was the last to rule the entire empire, and it was he, probably prompted by his mother, who legalised the Christian faith. He founded the city of Constantinople and built many churches there and in Rome and the Holy Land. His mother Helen, in her old age, made the pilgrimage to Jerusalem. There she ordered a search to be made at the site of Christ's crucifixion. Three crosses were found; which was the right one? A test was made, perfectly logical though hardly scientific. The true cross would surely have miraculous powers even to the extent of reviving a dead man, unlike those of the robbers. So it proved. The whole story can be read in the famous series of stained glass windows at Ashton-under-Lyne. The fame of the true cross, indeed fragments of it in unlikely quantity, spread throughout Christendom. Even here in Knutsford? Who knows.

The year 1741 was a bad one for the church in Knutsford. In January the steeple of St Helena's collapsed, and in the November following the tower of the parish church at Rostherne fell down too, as it had been threatening to do for years. These twin disasters prompted the reorganisation of the parish of Rostherne, and the former chapelry and town of Knutsford finally became a parish in its own right. A new parish church, St John's, was built on the tenterfield opposite the chapel

of ease, and both the chapels were dismantled. Meanwhile a fine new tower was built at Rostherne by Joseph Turner.

The First St Cross

So things remained until in 1858 a new church

was built for Crosstown for Higher Knutsford, dedicated to St Cross. It was a gaunt T-shaped edifice, with a gauche tower and spire, the design of which was said to have been by John Pennington Legh of Booths himself and the construction by Booths estate staff. Since the mansion had been recently much aggrandised by an architect called Edward Habershon it seems odd that Mr Legh should choose to go it alone, especially as the Leycesters at Toft had commissioned Habershon's brother, William Gilbee Habershon, to build their new church.

The motivation for the building of a new church so near St John's may have been a very long-standing grievance over the destruction of St Helena's, but it seems more likely that it was intended from the first to be 'higher' than St John's. This is indicated by the dedication; St Cross is a provocative dedication, smacking of idolatry to many. The dedication of Butterfield's church at Clayton in Manchester to St Cross in 1863 so infuriated Bishop Prince Lee that he refused altogether to consecrate it. It is a regrettable fact that churches of different persuasion do sometimes stoop slyly to provoking each other.

The first St Cross didn't last long. '*The building was far from beautiful architecturally, nor ecclesiastically all that could be desired, and although improvements almost amounting to restoration were effected during the (first) vicar's pastorate the Old Church was never very satisfactory as a place of worship.*' wrote the second vicar, Rev Ralph Bradbury. '*.... in the May of that year (1879) ominous fissures appeared from top to bottom of the walls, while the roof internally presented a complication of cracks in the plaster and externally resembled a well bent bow. An architect, after inspection, reported the building as being in an unsafe condition, the primary reason being that the wide span and excessive weight of the roof had thrust out the insufficiently solid walls*'. And so, after just twenty years, the first St Cross was taken down.

Is there anything left of it? The perimeter railings with their cross finials must date back to this first church. Inside the present church are a few memorials rescued from its predecessor. The materials must have been re-used, but not here; perhaps we should look in the neighbouring cottages and garden walls. I wonder if it could in fact have been saved. It is interesting to note the comments on its unsatisfactory nature as a place of worship, and also references to the new and wealthy residents brought in by the coming of the railway. Had the first St Cross simply become unfashionable?

Gothic was fashionable, but it had to be done properly. Church gothic of the time was

STX
Railings from first church.

concerned with accurate reproduction of medieval patterns, as at the contemporary St Philip's Alderley Edge for example. The first St Cross must have seemed much more old-fashioned than its actual age.

The Second St Cross

The foundation stone for an entirely new

church on the same site was laid by Lord Egerton of Tatton in July 1880. The architects this time were Messrs Austin and Paley of Lancaster. The church was to be in a free gothic, for the revival had by now passed the strictly imitative phase, and in brick and terracotta. The citizens of Crosstown were determined to have something up-to-date this time. Allowance was made for the church to be built in stages as the money came in; initially it had no tower top and no aisles, which must have looked very odd. They were added in 1887 and 1889 respectively to give us the church we see today. Austin and Paley's churches were often designed in this additive way but the cash to finish the job was not always forthcoming - see their St Mary Magdalene at Alsager for an unfortunate example. In the interval however the design of the tower top was changed radically from the original design which is shown on a drawing preserved at the church. The signature on the drawing proves that St Cross was actually the work of Hubert Austin.

Edmund Sharpe and the firm of Austin & Paley, Architects

The highly-respected firm of Austin and Paley had its HQ in Lancaster, in a handsome but plain Georgian house directly opposite the great frowning gate-tower of the Castle. For more than a hundred years a brass plate by the door announced their presence, although it had to be changed periodically as the different partners and generations succeeded one another. It was very much a family firm, literally so, for all the partners over the whole time that the practice was in being were closely related.

The founder of the firm was not an Austin nor a Paley, but Edmund Sharpe, a most interesting character, who was felicitously born in here Knutsford, just a stone's throw from St Cross.

Edmund Sharpe was born on Brook Street, in 1809, in a house which is currently and probably terminally boarded up, for it is just where the hill is narrowest and traffic most unpleasant. His father was the successful and jovial music master of the town and the organist at St John's; his mother Martha Whittaker was one of a great clan and ramification of Knutsford families, with branches in Lancaster among other places, that included Edmund's half-cousin and contemporary, Elizabeth Gaskell.

We can follow Master Sharpe's birth and early life in Knutsford from a series of letters written to and preserved by William Whittaker, Martha's nephew and so Edmund's cousin, later to be Vicar of Blackburn.

This was the age of wonderful letters. The recipient paid for the letter and so it behoved the sender to make sure it was worth paying for. So not only are we able to read the joyful news of young Edmund's birth and progress, we can get to know his parents and relations, and enjoy at almost two centuries' remove the social milieu and gossip of Knutsford.

The birth is announced by Thomas

Satterthwaite, writing to JW Whittaker at Sedburgh:-

Lancaster 15th Novr 1809

(I think he has mistaken the date - it must be the 16th at least)

'..... I am sorry I cannot have the pleasure of your company at present ... at Sedburgh. The distance from hence is 30 miles, a whole day's journey, over very bad road; so that in this cold weather, I should have but a miserable ride of it.

(a long learned discourse follows upon perspective and mathematics)

'You will, by this time, have heard, what grand doings there have been at Knutsford:- A couple of couzins ! Adieu ! Your's truly,

Thomas Satterthwaite'

The other 'couzin' was Charles Aikin Holland, born to Dr Peter Holland and his second wife Mary, Martha's sister.

Within a few days Martha Sharpe was feeling perky enough to write amusingly to her nephew, not just about her newborn son but about Brook Cottage as well:-

Nov 30th 1809

'Your letter, dear William, was very gratifying to me; not only as a proof of attention prompted I flatter myself by affection, but likewise as a specimen of greater ability in the epistolary way than most youths of your age can boast. Accept then my sincere thanks for it; & (as I am at frequent close housekeeping), received in good part a budget of home news, in return for the very hearty laughs many parts of your letter afforded me.

Be in the first place known to you, that your saucy epithet of 'Jacky' applies not to my little pet, who is to be named Edmund ...... let me tell you that my longings for anything have had no bad effect, for I never longed for anything but a dear healthy boy; & thank God, that (I hope) innocent longing has been so far fully satisfied.

Well now for your critique on the name of our Cot [Brook Cottage], which, to acquit your poor Mother of the charge of Romance, or some such term applied by you I must say was your Aunt Broadhurst's idea, & had its rise from the Brook which runs at the bottom of the garden [the Lily]. Perhaps it might be difficult to define the word cottage, which you very wisely think sometimes misapplied; but if the confines of the premises has anything to do with it, certainly this is a cottage, but thank God, it does not at present possess the usual appendages - dirt and want. You will I hope sometime or other experience that on the contrary it contains most of the comforts and blessings of life.

I believe the dear little fellow was hastened into the world at least a fortnight before he should have appear'd, by some hearty laughs, ... and the exertion of walking a good deal. But all this is of little moment, for he is a very promising boy, & seems to posess very perfect faculties. Of his beauties, Sally can sing with greater propriety than his modest Mama.

.... In a few months I fancy he will be work for everybody, for he promises to be very sharp by nature, as well as by name.

I am, dear Billy boy, your truly affectionate Aunt M.Sharpe'

She was right in her final surmise. He was. A letter from the music teacher a couple of years later gives us a vivid unconscious self-portrait of young Edmund's father, and of Knutsford society.

Knutsford 31st March 1812(?)

from Francis Sharpe, to William Whittaker at Cambridge.

'..... *In telling you all the news of this family, I conclude I must begin with all proper respect at the Top of the Tree; and I can do so with pleasure, for the old* Lady Oak *[he must mean his mother-in-law Anne Holland, nee Swinton, matriarch of the whole Holland clan and aged then about 72] is wonderful, and played her pool with her usual glee on Friday, when we took 'Tay' with her. I must say I never saw her in better health or spirits .....*

We have been uncommonly gay in Knutsford this winter - a Birthday Ball at 'Brook Cottage' *in honour of Mr "Little Man" - a concert at Miss Lumb's after, and danced about ten or twelve couples, and in the evening finished with a little spouting from some young ladies. A kind of Ball and supper at the Dutchman's [the Holland's] followed, and the chief amusement there was produced by Miss Wright, who sung and danced with the youngest - indeed why should she not - for she is in the market, and only sixty-two. On Thursday she will I fancy out-do all her doings, for we give a Hop here, to be composed of all the youngsters in town.*

Now master Billy, does not thy mouth water, or rather thy toes tingle, *or thy heels* fidget, *to be within reach of all this fun and frolic; or art thou so deep in the stick clay of* larning *that thou cannot step aside, even to view such folly in distant prospect? .... Now what say you to a Summer trip Northwards next July, or August, ...?'*

A postscript was added by Mrs Sharpe which gives the lie to the supposed inferior position of women at the time:-

'Well to be sure! - so I must needs take up my husband's pen - and what do I learn by it? - why, that he has been making all sorts of bargains & agreements & whatnots in my name, without my consent at all. Well now, pray who is master? Surely I am not expected to ratify this - how Magnanimous then shall I prove myself, in coming forward Voluntarily, *and adding my signature .... You cannot fancy a finer fellow than the little man has become - he walks by himself from room to room, & speaks many words .... My husband's pen is so very vile, that I cannot stumble on any longer - so, God bless you, dearest Willy, & believe me, ever yr affec Aunt, M Sharpe.'*

Actually 'dearest Willy' was turning into a rather po-faced young man. The Sharpes were prone to ribbing him.

In due course young Edmund, like his cousin Elizabeth, was sent away to school. He was of course required to write home every week, and occasionally to his other relations, while he was at school:-

Edmund Sharpe aged 17 from his school in Greenwich to Revd W Whittaker, Vicarage, Blackburn; in a fine copperplate script.

'*My dear cousin*

...... I have laid by my flute, and have determined

not to touch it again till I am in the sixth form. - I am certain of being the headboy on the 15th of October, whether I succeed in my trial or not. - I will give you a slight sketch of the exercises :-

We have to make a certain portion of Pindar, into 5 stanzas of Latin Aleaics: and to turn a portion of Latin prose selected from the "Scriptores Romani" in to 12 pairs of Hexameters and pure Iambics: a page of the history of Rome... (etc etc, a long list of academic exercises)

We are allowed a fortnight, and if we exceed that time, or if the number of our faults exceed 28, we fail, or as we term it 'spin'. We likewise fail if we have a single false concord, quantity, or inflexion in any of the exercises.

... I am glad you approve of the Sedburgh plan, I think it must be, from all accounts, a place well calculated for study.'

Elizabeth Gaskell describes just such a letter in 'Cranford':-

'It was very clear that the lad's were what are called show letters. They were of a highly mental description, giving an account of his studies, and intellectual hopes of various kinds, with an occasional quotation from the classics; but, now and then, the animal nature broke out in such a little sentence as this, evidently written in a trembling hurry, after the letter had been inspected: "Mother dear, do send me a cake, and put plenty of citron in."'

Edmund Sharpe went up from Sedburgh to Cambridge, where he came to the notice of that intellectual giant, and a great rock of a man, the Master of Trinity, William Whewell.

Although famed for his intellectual achievements a Cambridge legend describes how a well-known prize-fighter on meeting him exclaimed *"What a man was lost when they made you a parson!"*.

Whewell was born in obscurity in Lancaster, the son of a joiner. By a curious but pleasing coincidence, what must be one of the first intimations of his future greatness comes in a long and difficult-to-read post-script to Thomas Satterthwaite's letter, the very one already quoted which announces Edmund Sharpe's birth :-

'... We have a boy in this town of the name of Whewell who is quite a Prodigy of learning. He is a carpenter's son, and Mr Wilson of Dalham Tower has been interested to ?? him upon establishment at Heversham which will give him 46£ a year for collidge expenses for he is to go to your college, Trinity, I think ...'

William Whewell fostered an interest in gothic as the true architecture of the church, which was to result in Trinity being a training ground of Improving parsons, and not a few architects, fired up with the gothic revival. The Ecclesiological Society of Cambridge was to have an enormous influence on the course of architecture during the 19th century.

When Sharpe had gained his degree Whewell recommended that he apply for a travelling scholarship to the continent to study ancient architecture; which he successfully did. He spent three years touring the continent studying the Romanesque and the Gothic. He returned determined to be an architect. With supreme confidence he set himself up in practice in Lancaster, after spending a few days in the office of Thomas Rickman. This was the total extent of his technical training. Nor did he have to wait long for business, for the family mutual aid system sprang into action in the person of none other than his cousin the letter hoarder William Whittaker, now Vicar of the important parish of Blackburn.

Sharpe built eight churches for Whittaker, all before 1850, and was thus launched on a successful career. They are mostly in the Romanesque or Norman style, and are competent but not especially memorable. However he will always have at least a footnote in the history of architecture for his pot churches.

St Stephen's Lever Bridge, just outside Bolton, and Holy Trinity Platt which is next to Platt Hall in Manchester, plus St Paul's Scotforth in Lancaster, which was much later, are Edmund Sharpe's famous pot churches. Yes, they are indeed made out of pot, or terracotta as architectural pottery is more respectfully called. They are the result of the family mutual aid system again, this time that of his wife Elizabeth's family. The Fletchers owned a colliery at Lever Bridge which also yielded a good clay for terracotta. The churches were an attempt to use it on a large scale - partly experiment, partly advertisement. The experiment was only moderately successful at Lever Bridge, because the blocks were too large to fire through completely. Platt, built with smaller blocks, has fared very well, flourishing and still looking good. The terracotta is crisper than the local stone, conferring upon it a particular delicacy of outline and of detail.

But the Ecclesiologist hated them, and when the Ecclesiologist hated a new church it stayed hated, for that journal was perhaps the rudest magazine that has ever enjoyed respectability. This was unfortunate for Sharpe, a Cambridge graduate and protége of William Whewell, although he doesn't seem to have minded too much. They hated his pot churches because the terracotta pretends to be stone, a grand deception which should never be employed in any building let alone one dedicated to almighty God. All that lovingly hand-carved tracery and tooling was really cast in a factory in Bolton. Things that look like stone and wood are really pot. Disgraceful!

Edmund Sharpe's churches may tumble, even his pot churches may crumble, but his writings are here to stay. His great work published in 1848, the first of many, was called Architectural Parallels, a magnificent large folio of measured drawings and perspectives of the great abbeys of Fountains, Reivaulx, Kirkstall, Byland, Whitby etc, accompanied by a slimmer volume of mouldings drawn at full size. It must have been a huge effort and expense to survey all the buildings in their ruined state, to 'restore' the missing parts on paper, to prepare the stones for lithography and then pull the whole thing together for publication. It was to some extent, as it had to be, a team effort, and it is interesting to see from the plates that he was assisted by, among others, T Austin and EG Paley.

Settled in Lancaster Edmund Sharpe soon developed interests outside architecture, so much so that it is hard to think of any aspect of provincial town life that he did not contribute to. He became involved with local politics on a platform of sanitary reform, serving as mayor in 1848. He founded the Lancaster Rowing club, was a notable member of the cricket club, and an accomplished archer. He was the founder of the choral society and their conductor for some time, and the manager of the Athenaeum. At the same time he became interested in the promotion of railways, and soon found himself not only on boards of directors but acting as contractor and engineer for some of the schemes he had helped to promote. He was the contractor for the first few bridges south of Lancaster on the present west coast main line. He was the chief promoter, then Company Secretary, and finally supplier of locomotives and rolling stock to a line called the Little North Western which connected Skipton in Yorkshire with Lancaster and on to the new coastal town of Morecambe. It had the highest ambitions, a major port at Morecambe and international traffic to Ireland. In the event it was a pretty ramshackle concern, not the least of its problems being Mr Sharpe's incompetent engineering, but it did create a curious social anomaly in that Morecambe's roots are all with Leeds and Derby and not at all with its Lancashire hinterland.

By 1851 Edmund Sharpe had formally quit the practice of architecture. He took into partnership and then handed over to Edward Paley. This was the same EG Paley of 'Architectural Parallels', who married Sharpe's sister Frances in 1851. Paley in turn took on Hubert Austin. Austin, half brother of the T Austin who prepared so many of the stones for 'Architectural Parallels', married in 1870 Fanny, daughter of Edmund Sharpe's sister Emily. The firm and its work was all in the family from first to last. Leisure time was no different; it is recorded that the rowing four of the Lancaster Rowing Club usually consisted of Sharpe, Paley, Austin and one other, and that they were all actively involved in local music-making and in the life of Lancaster Priory.

Following his railway works in Lancaster Sharpe was the builder of the Conwy valley line up from the Junction to Llanrwst, and was part-owner of a line in the south of France. He died in 1877, suddenly and unexpectedly, in Milan where he was again studying medieval architecture.

Edward Paley, who took over the firm from Sharpe, was a master of true medieval gothic, and his architecture is a convincing recreation of it. A major work is St Peter's Bolton; a splendid landmark and a fine evocation of the middle ages; but dull. The old church was much more characterful. Another fine work is St Peter's catholic church, now cathedral, in Lancaster. Nearer to home is Davenham church with its very tall spire.

Greatness came to the firm with Hubert Austin; it was the practice's golden age. That is the received wisdom. He was not an imitator like Paley but an original, able to create new forms on the basis of traditional styles. His masterwork is St George's, Stockport, which is worthy to be a cathedral. The almost unlimited funds to build it were given by Mr Fearn, a brewer, whose grave is marked by a delightful model of the steeple. St George's was locally nicknamed 'Fearn's Fire Insurance', because Mr Fearn had led rather a gay life and was conscience stricken.

Nobility and resourcefulness are the characteristics Pevsner attributes to Hubert Austin. Personally I admire his works more than I like them. I can see that they are fine, I can appreciate the special awareness, the calculated asymmetries, the unusual lighting effects. But I find his churches peculiarly opaque and dispiriting, the world shut out by clouded glass and dense tracery and the light struggling always with his favourite red sandstone or brick. I was amused to find that the only red brick house in Lancaster, a town blessed with an inexhaustible supply of excellent creamy grey stone, was Hubert Austin's. I also dislike some of his inventiveness. His pier shapes and capitals can be horrid - see those of the King's Own memorial chapel in Lancaster Priory with their undecipherable black-letter inscriptions snaking round the capitals.

St Cross in Knutsford belongs to the golden age of Austin & Paley and exemplifies all Hubert Austin's virtues, and his faults.

Austin wanted St Cross to have a strong central tower, always an effective form from the outside. It is a challenge structurally because it has to be raised up on arches; a huge weight standing over empty space. Because of the tower poised above it it is difficult to make the central space anything other than dark and constricted, just where you don't want a dark and constricted space. The effect is seen clearly at Stafford parish church, and at Nantwich; at both of these churches the altar has been brought forward, not just for liturgical reasons but because the old one at the east end is obscured by the fat columns of the crossing.

Austin has solved this problem triumphantly at St Cross. There are no transepts but instead low aisles whose end walls are sufficient to brace the tower transversely. Above the aisle roofs he has contrived huge windows which flood the crossing with light, so that the space under the tower, normally the darkest part of the church, is the brightest. From the west end the blaze of light at the crossing is very good. The whole design of St Cross centres round this idea.

He then throws away the effect by glazing it with dingy frosted glass, and by the bald dark red brickwork of the tower space.

Spatially however, the most stunning effect of St Cross church Knutsford is invisible to the ordinary worshipper. All churches have hidden spaces, narrow turning stairs leading up to roof spaces, ringing chambers and tower tops. Austin needed to provide access to his central tower, but it is impossible to put a turning stair in one of the four columns that carry it without weakening it, or without thickening it up and so restricting the view. Master masons and architects through the centuries have had fun solving this problem. Anyone who has been up the great central tower at Salisbury will know that you start the ascent right at the other end of the cathedral and wind your way upwards via breathtaking galleries and wondrous roof spaces, only getting to the tower itself at rooftop level. Here at St Cross Hubert Austin has played a nice little private game. There is a tiny door in the outer wall of the church by the lady chapel. A few turning stairs leads up to a short iron ladder, and at the top of that is a straight and narrow transverse stairway lit by the occasional tiny slit window - just like something in a Norman castle. The amazing coup here is its incredible length. It goes on and on, and up and up, much further than can be possible, surely.....

The trick is that he has taken you from the outer wall of the aisle right across the church to the far corner of the tower in one straight run. I feel sure that this was the real driving force of the design, rather than the more obvious device of the tower windows. I can imagine him chortling over his drawing board; an effect almost prefiguring Escher, but seen by nobody.

The interior of St Cross is distinguished by two stained glass windows by William Morris & Co, one in the South transept and an exceptionally fine one, very broad rather than tall, at the west end. It commemorates Lieutenant Percy Walton Galloway who died at Agra in India on the 22nd of April 1893 aged 27. The window was given by his parents Charles John and Annie Galloway of Thorneyholme.

Thorneyholme has gone. It was a big showy house in Manor Park, built in 1885, with timber-framing in the upper floors and lots of tall twisty chimneys. Two lodges remain. The East Lodge shows by its over-complicated geometry and especially by the fierce carved animals that slaver from underneath the bay windows the mind of a roguish architect. Alfred Darbyshire very likely, who lived nearby and who designed the library. Thorneyholme was nicknamed by the younger members of the family 'Biler 'all', because the family business at Knott Mill and Ardwick was boilers. Also steel; Charles' father John Galloway had been a close friend and business partner of Henry Bessemer, allowing him to carry out his first trials in steelmaking at the Knott Mill works.

The Galloways were generous supporters of St Cross church, as they were also at Mobberley. 'Biler 'all' housed a notable contemporary art collection. One of Mr Galloway's best pictures was 'The Roll Call' by

Miss Thompson, later Lady Butler; a realistic scene of the Crimean war, not heroic but compassionate. It caused a sensation at the Royal Academy and was, by Royal command, sent down to Osborne. Her Majesty liked it so much she leaned on Mr Galloway to part with it, which he gallantly did. And so it is now in the Royal collection.

The final object to merit our attention at St Cross takes us right back to the time of St Helena's or even earlier. In the porch of the church is a rude and barbaric lump of carved stone, battered and cracked through. It is supposed to be an ancient cross base that was found either nearby or at the site of St Helena's. At some time it has been converted to a font by the enlargement of the cross socket into a lead-lined bowl, although the fearsome monsters that scowl and leer from its corners would hardly inspire confidence in that sacrament.

This great stone is parked immovably in the corner of the porch so that you can only see two sides of it. A nice bunch of flowers in the bowl distracts you from looking at it closely, and in any case the carvings are right down at floor level. I do wonder if this is entirely accidental, because it really is a frightening thing. Who knows what the monsters on the other two sides are like? The ones we can see are bad enough. Is it really a cross base? Are those angel's wings or bat's wings?

A bottom corner of ? Cross.

STX
12th May 2000
M.H.

Site of St Helena

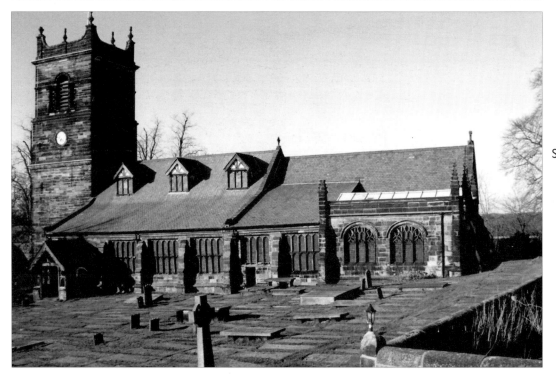

St Mary's Rostherne

St Cross Church in its first incarnation lasted little more than twenty years, from 1858-1879

Brooke Cottage - the birthplace of Edmund Sharpe.

universal knowledge of Perspective. You will, by this time, have heard what grand doings have been at Knutsford:— A couple of cousins!

Adieu! Yours Truly,

Thomas Satterthwaite

Letter of 15/11/1809 recording the birth of Edmund Sharpe and Charles Holland.

Edmund Sharpe's Horse

School letter from.
Edmund Sharpe 7/9/1826.

I will give you a slight sketch of the exercises;

We have to make a certain portion of Pindar, into 5 stanzas of Latin Alcaics: and from to turn a portion of Latin prose selected from the "Scriptores Romani" into 12 pairs of Hexameters and pure Iambics: a page of the History of Rome to translate into Latin Prose: an English translation from any Latin prose writer, the same from any Greek prose writer, of each not less than 20 lines. Three pages of the latter part of Huntingford's Greek Exercises to rectify. One of

The Sharpe family move[d] from Brook House to Heathfield, which has go[ne] This small farm stood ne[xt] to it.

A beautiful example of th[e] stained glass work of Morris & Co, the west window of St Cross is a memorial to Percy Walto[n] Galloway, who died in Ind[ia] in 1898, aged 26.

...evaulx Abbey, a
...awing prepared
...r Edmund Sharpe's
...rchitectural Parallels'
... Edward Paley.

...r right:
...rracotta detail at
...inity Church, Platt.

...St Pauls Scotforth, with
...ore terracotta detail.

Holy Trinity Church, Platt in Manchester.

Crisp-detail in terracotta.

Terracotta 'carving' grained to look like wood from a pew end at Holy Trinity, Platt - Edmund Sharpe's 'pot church'.

Relics of Edmund Sharpe's 'Little' North Western Railway.

Top: Lune bridge, one of a pair.

Below: Site of Green Ayre Station, with the railway bridge in the background.

Messrs Austin & Paley's offices by Lancaster Cas Lancaster owes much of dignity to the firm, which was founded by Edmund Sharpe of Knutsford.

Hubert Austin's house in Lancaster, incongruous in red brick.

Stained glass studios of Messrs Shrigley and Hunt at Lancaster.

H Austin watercolour   *Courtesy Lancaster Library*

Shrigley & Hunt's studio incorporates examples of their work. The firm was Austin and Paley and as much used by them.

The second St Cross and its vicarage today.

MR. CHARLES J. GALLOWAY, J.P.
(From a Photo by Mr. Arthur Reston, Stretford.)

Interior of the second St Cross from the east end.

LANCASHIRE INDUSTRIES.
GALLOWAYS LIMITED, MANCHESTER. CENTRAL BAY OF BOILER WORKS.
(From a Photo.)

he Galloway residence,
horneyholme, stood not far from
Cross. Known disrespectfully as
iler 'all' due to the family business,
l that remains today are the two
dges.

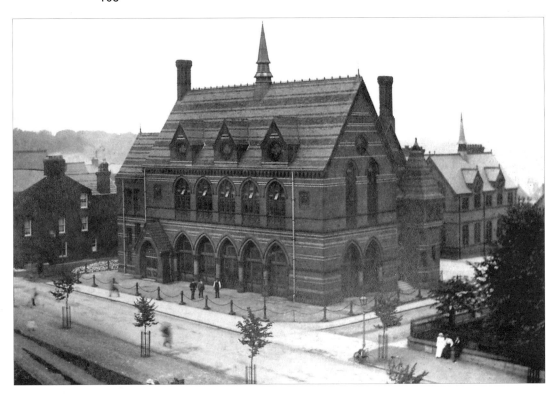

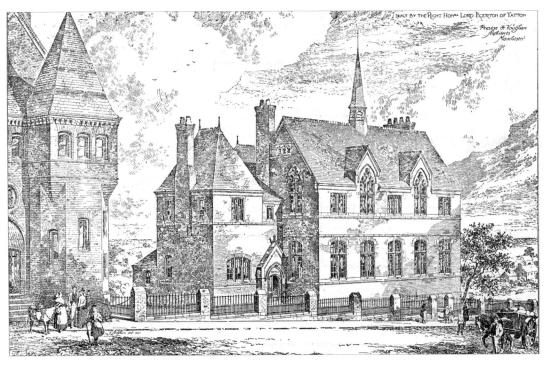

Five

THE TOWN HALL AND EGERTON SCHOOL

Alfred Waterhouse, Lord Egerton, and the Town Hall 1871 - the school and Wilbraham Egerton - the army hut - the Donut Dugout and General Patton's gaffe - the Boys Club and 'Lordy', the last Lord Egerton.

It is commonly called the town hall but it was not built by the town. It has never belonged to the town, nor is there much evidence that the town needed such a thing. It was never an administrative centre for a town council. Today it houses a furniture store and, in unlikely juxtaposition, the post office. How can we explain this very dominating but seemingly unwanted building?

The foundation stone, usually hidden by furniture, explains:-
THIS • MARKET • HOUSE • WAS • ERECTED • BY • WILLIAM • TATTON • BARON • EGERTON • OF • TATTON • WHO • LAID • THIS • STONE • APRIL • 4 • 1872 •

The market hall was intended to be open at the front, hence the blue pillars. Upstairs was a large room for assemblies and concerts. At the back a couple of small meeting rooms and a caretaker's flat. That is all.

Architecturally speaking Knutsford Town Hall is a most unsuitable building for such a nice town. It would be much more at home in a tough district of Manchester or Stockport. It pays no attention to the genius of the place, ignoring its neighbours in size and shape, in colour and texture, and in its style and materials. It must have stood out like a sore thumb when it was built, so red, so tall, so gothic, so stripy. Its architect was one whose works often created a considerable reaction when they first went up, not all of it favourable:-

That Prudential man Alfred Waterhouse
used to tell all his clients he thought a house
should be partly chateau
and partly gateau
but chiefly municipal slaughterhouse.

(Punch)

I am reminded of his St Paul's School in London which right up to its demolition in the 1968 made a powerful impact even in a frenetically urban environment; but when first built near the village of Hammersmith, looming up over the lane and the cottages, it must have seemed as though beings from another planet had landed. Waterhouse was not one for sensitivity to the neighbours.

He was, however, a great architect. Knutsford Town Hall does not show him at his best, but the evidence for his greatness is there if you care to look. His best buildings are his biggest: Manchester Town Hall, the Natural History Museum in London, Manchester University and Museum, and, I dare say, Strangeways prison. He was good at a big strong church as well, like St Elisabeth's, Reddish, although being a Quaker, like Alfred Darbyshire, he did little church work. He was quite incapable of doing anything cosy, or sweet, or comforting.

That said, he had everything requisite for greatness and success. He was an excellent artist, exhibiting annually at the Royal Academy; his architectural perspectives are worth looking at just for their incidental street life and beautiful skies. He thought in three dimensions, not a universal accomplishment among architects; so his buildings look good from all angles, not just flat on. He was a virtuoso at staircases, and street corners, and roof spaces, and decorative ironwork, as a tour of Manchester Town Hall will verify. He was especially good at planning a complex building with potentially conflicting functions, such as a courthouse. Public and Press entering a court would never come face to face with the Jury retiring in a Waterhouse court, as happens in the Sessions House opposite. He had a sure colour sense; this might seem a contradiction to the 'slaughterhouse' epithet but his stained glass and tiled floors are most unusual for the period for their quiet control. He was industrious and trustworthy, keeping to time and within the budget. He had moreover a winning smile, and influential relations in the law and accountancy. What more could a man want? Sensitivity perhaps.

So we can pick out the good qualities. Despite its harshness Knutsford Town Hall is magnificent streetscape, composing well from all angles and having a splendidly dramatic skyline. Inside it seems at first barn-like and distinctly unloved, but the staircase is good, a stone cantilever supported on a couple of iron girders. The decorative railings are well worth noting although the cast iron newels are frankly monstrous.

Not many Victorian architects would have exposed the structural beams, but he was interested in construction and, unlike most of his prudish contemporaries, was happy to demonstrate it. The roof is the main feature of the assembly hall. Slender iron ties pull it

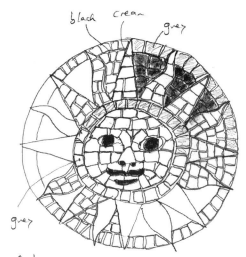

black cream
grey
grey

M/C Uni Grad stair floor. 1884
16 June 2000 MH.

together, with flat discs at the joins. From the little orchestra gallery these discs can be seen to be suns, with rays alternately straight and wavy, and a smily face on each one. Comical and surprising; but where have I seen one before? Of course, in the University of Manchester coat of arms, ARDUUS AD SOLEM, the snake of the Cavendishes and the sun a symbol of pure enlightenment. The university has both Egerton and Waterhouse connections, for it was built by Alfred Waterhouse on Egerton land. Perhaps the most astonishing feature of Knutsford Town Hall is that Waterhouse managed to give any attention to it at all given that he had three or even four massively complex jobs on at the same time:- Manchester Town Hall, Eaton Hall near Chester for the Grosvenors, and the Natural History Museum in London, not to mention finishing the first building for Owen's College -

Manchester University today.

Waterhouse ignored the Knutsford milieu, and his town hall stood for twenty years isolated by its uncompromising style. But in 1893 round the corner in Church Street arose an equally good building which took its cue from the town hall, creating a little group of spiky Victoriana. This is Egerton School, not by Waterhouse but by a firm called Preston and Vaughan of Manchester. It is in the same style, copying its general outline and many of its details, but it has less of the feel of a big fish in a little pond, and is the better for it. Furthermore it forgoes the stripes and some of the more aggressive modelling.

The boys had the big schoolroom downstairs, entered by the left hand door, and the girls had the more airy room upstairs, entering by the right hand door and going up the broad shallow staircase fitted with brass knobs to discourage sliding down the banisters. At one end was the schoolteacher's house, and in the yard, also divided into boys' and girls' sections, were the outside toilets. It is all pretty basic, with bare painted brick and bare floorboards, stoves or fireplaces and a big vent in the roof to let out the stink of children, but spacious and solid to use and a fine building to look at.

'These schools' proclaims a large iron plate in the downstairs schoolroom, 'were erected by WILBRAHAM BARON EGERTON OF TATTON to secure all parents in Knutsford the existing advantages of Religious Education and secular instruction in the training of their children'.

Wilbraham Egerton was something of an architect himself. He added the yellow terracotta extensions to Tatton Hall; not actually a great advertisement for his architectural talent.

A worthwhile comparison can be made with the town centre of nearby Sandbach where there is a much more complete group of civic and public buildings all given or sponsored by the great landowning family. These were the Crewes of Crewe Hall, but they didn't do much for Crewe. The building in the Sandbach group that looks like Knutsford Town Hall - same mood, style, colour and size - is the Literary Institute of 1854, which is by Gilbert Scott who was an even busier man than Waterhouse. Next to it and supporting it are a Savings Bank, encouraging thrift as the Literary Institute encouraged self-education, and two fine inns. Nearby is the rebuilt grammar school. The Town Hall that completes the group was built in 1889 by a local architect, Thomas Bower, and is altogether more friendly-looking than either the Literary Institute or Knutsford Town Hall. Unlike Knutsford it is still fulfilling its original functions - market stalls below, public hall above.

Most schools, however spacious and well-planned at the outset, acquire a mobile classroom, usually a place distinctly substandard, out of sight and out of mind. In the case of Egerton School the 'mobile' is perhaps

the most interesting building on the site. It looks like a venerable First World War army hut. This is the sort of unregarded building whose survival thus far can only be due to pure chance. Who knows what stories it has to tell?

The old town hall in Knutsford has one place in world history; or perhaps it would be truer to say it very nearly did have. And it would have been a disastrous one. The story is worth telling in some detail.

During the Second World War huge numbers of troops trained in Tatton Park in the relatively new technique of parachuting. That story is told in the Tatton Old Hall chapter.

In the lead up to D-Day, in 1944, a new element came into the picture in the form of the American Third Army, under its charismatic commander, General George Patton. This force was actually assembled and made into a new fighting force in the area around Knutsford. Patton himself took over Peover Hall, where he lived, with all his staff, in considerable style. This was the command post. Officers were housed in big houses as far away as Alderley Edge and the men encamped and trained wherever space could be found. The American Third Army was a very smart concern, for Patton was a stickler for appearances.

It all had to be a big secret though. 'I am not here', Patton was wont to say, 'and nor are you'. Under the deception plan called 'Fortitude' a dummy Third Army assembled in the southeast of England ready for mythical landings at Calais; the whole was given substance by fake tanks and encampments, bogus radio traffic, and diversionary air raids so persuading, it was hoped, the enemy to concentrate his defenses in the wrong place.

The whole plan almost went astray, and Patton nearly got the sack at just the time when he was most needed, because of a laughable incident at Knutsford in April 1944 just six weeks before D-Day. Two clubs were set up by the ladies of Knutsford, intended to provide some home comforts and social contacts for the GIs. The Friendship Club was at the Ruskin Rooms, for officers, and here at the town hall was the Donut Dugout for the men.

General Patton himself was asked to declare them open. He agreed to appear, insisting however that there should be no press and no photographs. In vain, for he was highly newsworthy. The press were there, and they reported an appalling gaffe in his impromptu speech, given the extremely critical stage of the war and the sensitivity of relations between the Allies. 'After the war' was his gist, 'America and Britain will rule the world, so we might as well get to know each other'. This was I suppose a reasonable thing to say in a small British town at a purely local function, but in the world press the omission of the Soviet Union as future world rulers was a dreadful indiscretion. Patton was summoned to London and severely reprimanded by Eisenhower. It was a crushing blow. The mutual friendship and trust between them was never the same again. But he was not relieved of his command, as some of Eisenhower's aides urged, and went on to lead his Third Army to glory in the last stages of the war. Without his leadership - and he and Montgomery were undoubtedly the finest leaders amongst the Allied forces - things could have take a different turn altogether.

After the war the town hall was returned to the Egertons. Maurice, Lord Egerton, or 'Lordy' as he was disrespectfully called, started a boy's club in the old place that was a model of its kind, and is still going strong although no longer in this building. He had also given the boys a 25 acre field by the park, which is where the new clubhouse was built. The club was run by 'Skip' Waite for many years, then Eric Ball, and many will remember the old bus 'Ivanhoe' that took them for holidays or excursions or the annual walk back from Chester.

Maurice was a familiar figure in and around Knutsford, small and rather disreputable-looking, shy but tough. Those who thought they knew him - and he was an enigmatic man - only knew the half of his life. The other half was in Kenya, where perhaps his heart was. At Njoro, a hundred miles to the northwest of Nairobi in the White Highlands, he had a vast estate. There was a big and rather ugly house - locals called it the castle - complete with a duplicate of the huge tenants' hall he had built at Tatton and, like it, equipped with a player organ. Lord Egerton did not play the organ himself but loved to run the rolls. The house is now somewhat ruinous, though still in use, but the great estate has become Egerton University.

Maurice Egerton was fond of boy's toys. His motor car, M1, was the first to be registered in Cheshire, and he was a pioneer in flying and in radio. He was a game hunter on a compulsive scale; a crack shot, fearless and tough, a real boy's own hero. Every kill was meticulously recorded in his game book, and hundreds of specimens were sent back to the taxidermist in England to be stuffed and mounted. Some were presented to the Manchester Museum where they can be seen still, beautiful but sad. Others line the walls of the tenant's hall. Just as game hunting has passed, hopefully, out of fashion for ever so the trophies of the hunt have become distasteful to us. He was very anxious that his own trophies should be preserved, labelled correctly, and made available for the education and edification of the public. Presenting us today with something of a problem.

Knutsford Town Hall has been much neglected of late; the fact that it is still basically sound is a tribute to its architect and to its builders, J Parnell & Sons. It can never be a lovable building but it is worthy of preservation and a more dynamic use.

MH 15 June 2000
Old Town Hall.

Above:
Alfred Waterhouse
monogram, and Alfred
Waterhouse.

Above far right:
Maurice, Lord Egerton

Egerton of Tatton initials
in the glass leading of
the school.

The upper floor of the Town Hall is a single space that was intended to be used as an assembly room

This unassuming hut in the playground of Egerton School, used as a mobile classroom, may date back to the First World War.

May Day 2000 and no cars for two blissful hours, thus enabling the author to pose in front of the Town Hall.

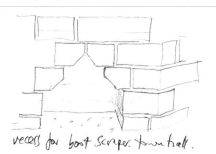

recess for boot scraper town hall.

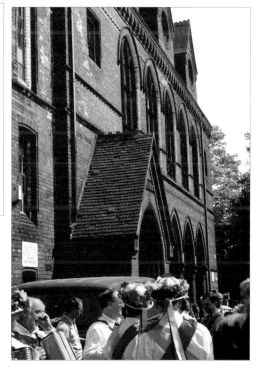

Gate Tower.   White Tower.   Bell Tower.

Knutsford Sanitary Laundry.   Oct 8 . 1900 —
            from Stonier's field. —   5 P.M. —

Six
RICHARD HARDING WATT

Critical press - his travels and business - comes to Knutsford 1897 - Drury Lane - collaboration with Fairhurst - the Legh Road villas - later collaborators - the Ruskin Rooms and the influence of Ruskin - the Belle Epoque - large scale picturesque design - his death. Watt's sources. Latter-day comparisons:- Portmeirion, Les Oakes's Yard.

Local people enjoy the works of Watt, but he has never been considered seriously as an architect. Hear what Pevsner has to say, in the Cheshire volume (1971) of his magisterial 'Buildings of England'.

'the maddest sequence of villas in all England' - Legh Road. He didn't like them at all. '*.... his remorseless imposing of crazy grandeur on poor Knutsford*' - the Gaskell Memorial Tower and Coffee House, now the Belle Epoque. *'perpetrated'* referring to the Ruskin Rooms. Nikolaus Pevsner had the ability to destroy a building's reputation with a single word.

Like them or not, Watt has made his mark on Knutsford. His are the most distinctive buildings in town, unmistakable in their Mediterranean whiteness and their inventive use of second-hand materials and wayward inscriptions. Anyway, whatever the critics say he has been given the ultimate accolade of being much imitated, if in diluted form.

Richard Watt only came to Knutsford late in life, and his buildings were all created in just ten years.

In his earlier life he was an adventurer. He was born in 1842 of South African parents, and is thought to have had interests in the South African gold mines. In 1864, in his early twenties, he took passage to Australia on the sailing ship 'Young Australia' carrying emigrants. They set sail from Gravesend in early May, and he describes the taking on of possessions including many musical instruments. Only two days later a woman in steerage was confined - 'our first birth'. The ship carried livestock which was butchered en route for fresh meat. On 15 June they crossed the equator, with many pranks accompanying the arrival on board of King Neptune in person, but at the end of July the ship was blown off course by a mighty storm. They finally arrived at the mouth of the Brisbane river on 13 August. Over the next two days the passengers and all their belongings were taken ashore on a stern-wheeler. Watt describes it all in a journal, illustrated with his own sketches, which is now preserved in the Mitchell library in Sydney. In later years he travelled to Switzerland, Corsica, Spain, Morocco and Algeria, to Scandinavia, to America, to Palestine and Egypt, and to India, always keeping a journal and making sketches. Some of his travels were for the purpose of buying suitable leather for his business, which was Richard Watt & Co, glove manufacturer, listed at 7 Piccadilly, Manchester, and at 11 Milk Street London and 70 Miller Lane Glasgow. He was especially fond of Italy - who isn't? - and seems to have had particular links with the north Italian lakes, Como, Maggiore and Lugano.

In 1895 Richard Watt started to build himself a house in Legh Road Knutsford called The Croft. It was a good solid house in an Arts-and Crafts style, but nothing special. It was designed by John Brooke, a former neighbour in Bowdon. Brooke was involved in the development of the lands sold off by the Leghs of Booths, following the coming of the railway; it may be that it was he who suggested the move. We can imagine Watt being fascinated by the building of his house and tiresomely interfering at every stage. Always interested in stones and bricks, in the picturesque possibilities of buildings, and the opportunity for improving the world on his own terms, he became gripped by the mania to build which has been the undoing of many a one through the ages. He had the means, he was able to acquire the land, he had a ready market, he

even appears to have been blessed with an acquiescent town council and tolerant neighbours. At all events he achieved in an astonishingly short time a transformation of his adopted town such as few could have imagined.

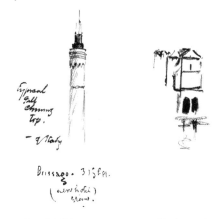

In 1897, starting small, he altered the appearance of a row of cottages at the bottom of his land, Croft Cottages, with some timbering, pantiles and fancy chimneys. The following year he built an entirely new house, Moorgarth, and in 1899 he bought and started to transform an old tannery in the town into a model laundry.

In all these works he needed an intermediary, who would see to it that the buildings were sound and would stand up. Watt had no architectural training. He was a good topographical artist but was never able to work happily with plans and elevations, preferring to use models. John Brooke was too well established, with ideas of his own, to serve as Watt's ghost. He needed someone young and untried, trained in the techniques of architecture but submissive to his ideas. He lighted on Harry S Fairhurst, a young and ambitious architect from Blackburn, who ghosted all these first works. Fairhurst, born in 1868, had risen through his own efforts from grocer's boy, where he used to make arches in the window display out of bags of tea, to an architectural training at the age of twenty with Messrs Maxwell and Tuke who were building Blackpool Tower at the time, and Associateship of the RIBA.

Watt needed to communicate to young Fairhurst his enthusiasm for all things Italian, and he wanted Fairhurst to study at first hand the minutiae and constructional details of the features he liked. So in 1898 he took him to Italy, though Fairhurst insisted on paying his own way as far as he was able. It was not a leisurely trip. Fairhurst's sketchbooks are full of little annotated drawings of chimneys and balconies entitled 'from train'. He appears to have covered a lot of ground.

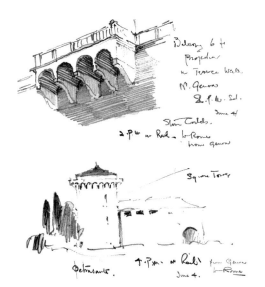

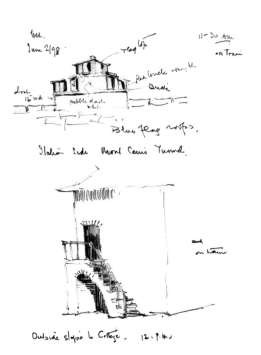

The old tannery buildings stretched down the length of the narrow Drury Lane from King Street to the watery Moor. It was a site with eminent possibilities for the picturesque and one that could be admired from the open land across the lane, from the Moor, and even from the embanked railway, although it was to take Watt ten years to realise these possibilities fully.

A laundry, moreover, was a sound business proposition and it offered the opportunity for some social engineering. Watt followed closely the ideas of John Ruskin; not only on the subject of stones and of gothic and landscape, but in the concept of the dignity of work and the importance of providing good housing and the opportunity for self-improvement. All these came together, in time, at the laundry on Drury Lane.

A laundry needs its own water supply. Goody, a tower. It needs boilers; aha, nice round shapes. A tall chimney will be required. Hmm, now that's rather industrial, but if it were to be disguised as a minaret .....

In the end Watt and Fairhurst achieved a wonderfully picturesque composition stepping down the hill, all white, with an exotic oriental-looking skyline and entertaining detail at every scale, from the balconies fronting the workers' cottages and the tricky brickwork of their garden walls to the tiny smiling face in the hinge of the laundry gate. Watt couldn't resist a permanent exhortation and a quote :- LET YOUR GARMENTS ALWAYS BE WHITE, from the book of Ezekiel apparently, which was set in

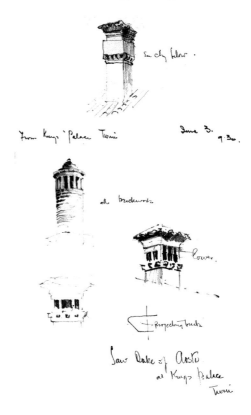

glazed brick in the watertower minaret .

It is not to be expected that Harry Fairhurst would suffer Richard Watt's dictatorial ways for long, nor that he should be prepared to carry the can for the failings resulting from Watt's insistence on Italian methods in Knutsford. Smoking chimneys were the final breaking point, which occurred in 1901. He was soon launched on his own very successful career in Manchester in which the influence of Watt is nil. Many of the huge warehouses that line Whitworth Street are his. The Fairhurst practice is still with us, in the person of Harry M Fairhurst the grandson of the founder.

The next collaborator employed by Watt was Walter Aston of Bollington. Aston had his own quirky style of architecture - see his overcomplicated Fence Almshouses at the bottom of Buxton Road in Macclesfield - but it is not at all like Watt. First came White Howe or the White House of 1901. Moorgarth, next door, had been fairly conventional, although it now has a somewhat Japanesy look to it with thin decoration in wood. It seems largely unrelated to his later work. White Howe is definitely Italianate, with its Roman pantiles (actually they were made in Bridgwater Somerset) set on wide hipped roofs, and its rough render overall, which Watt must have hoped would peel picturesquely as it does in the hot Italian sun, instead of going mouldy as it tends to do in Knutsford. The house could also be called Romanesque with its suggestion of a pele tower at one end and its round arches. It is set above a series of terraces linked by steps which gradually run into the wilderness of Sanctuary Moor, as recommended in Edith Wharton's 'Italian Villas and their Gardens'. This was first published in 1904 but it is quite possible that she and Watt were acquainted and knew of each other's ideas, having a common enthusiasm. '*He should remember*' she enjoins in her opening chapter, 'Italian garden-magic', '*that the terraces and formal gardens adjoined the house, that the ilex or laurel walks beyond were clipped into shape to effect the transition between the straight lines of masonry and the untrimmed growth of the woodland to which they led, and that each step away from architecture was a nearer approach to nature.*'

White Howe is conventionally planned for the time in its provision of segregated accommodation. The service quarters with their back stair are grouped at the north end of the house, demarcated from the rest of the house by a 'green baize' door, and the family quarters are provided with a good front stair lit by a tall window, drawing room and dining room, bedrooms with dressing rooms, and a nursery suite in the attic. But Watt avoids the conventional double plan. White Howe is only one room deep, with the hallway running through from front to back. This means that the house is not nearly as big as it appears from the road. None of the rooms are large but they are unusually well lit, with most rooms windowed on two sides. The dining room and the bedroom above it have pleasant semicircular bows overlooking the garden and Sanctuary Moor.

The house is probably built of reclaimed bricks - there are plenty more about the garden. The coat of Italian render made this a viable option though it was not at all the done thing for a respectable railway villa. Watt would have seen an enormous amount of urban renewal in Manchester - not least for Harry Fairhurst's new warehouses. He must have hated to see the old materials go to waste.

A few reclaimed fragments are used in an architectural way - four semicircular arches with keystones, perhaps originally over the fanlights of a row of Georgian houses, are used and there is an engaging lantern to the service stair which is cobbled up of some square balusters with tiny windows inserted between them. Inside the house the hall floor is a fine inlaid piece made up of individual squares of patterned wood - more of the same appear at Lake House. I suspect the main stair is reclaimed but Watt has discarded the fussy turned balusters in favour of chunky white-painted uprights of plain square section such as Voysey might have used.

Next came Lake House, originally Tor Walden, which is dated 1903. This is a much more ambitious house. Lake House is built at right angles to the road, so that the passer-by sees only the kitchen end, livened by a shallow bay and an inscription. The visitor however would drive in by the carriageway at the further end of the plot, where a motor house, now called Breeze and in separate ownership, was soon to be built, to be confronted by the full spectacular length of the house stretched out down the hill and facing due south. The idea of building this house at right angles may have been born of good neighbourliness, for it allows the house on the other side of the road to retain its view. It also allows the passer-by a glimpse over Sanctuary Moor, and it gives variety to the whole group of his villas which by now were taking shape in his head.

White Howe was in design and construction quite simple; a single block with a straightforward footprint, diversified by some variations in the roof height and a single semicircular bay. Lake House is much more complicated. It is composed of three contrasting units - a rectangular block nearest to the road, roofed in Watt's favourite Roman pantiles; an L-shaped flat-roofed section; and a massive round tower. A second smaller round tower links the pantiled and the flat-roofed sections.

Such a complex plan could easily be a mess, but the planning of the interior follows these three sections logically and it seems to work very well both practically and aesthetically. The pantiled block is the service section plus the dining room. The flat-roofed section is for circulation, containing the main stairs linking a spacious reception hall to an open billiard room below and topped with a sun terrace. The round tower stacks up on four floors a study, drawing room, bedroom and what is called the tower room, really a bit of fun.

There are no boring rooms in Lake House. The presence of the two round towers and the shallow bay at the road end, combined with the joins between the different sections and the fall of the land, have allowed Watt really to enjoy himself. The visitor experiences a sequence of visual and spatial delights, reinforced by the endless variety in detail such as window furniture and fireplaces. We enter the house through a small circular lobby, cool and echoey; are then welcomed into a spacious reception hall with a warm inlaid wood floor (reclaimed, see White Howe) and an excellent copper fire surround of Art Nouveau inspiration. The room is L-shaped with the stairs rising and descending from the upstroke, and is lit from two sides: brightly from the sunny front of the house, more subdued but golden from the tall window at the back. Downstairs is an even more pleasing room, because unexpected and because you descend

into it. The fall of the ground allows it to be fully lit from three sides, and it actually manages to be bigger than the hall - there must be some structural juggling to support the walls above. This splendid room has no formal function which makes it more enjoyable still - games room, garden room, retreat.

Over a Rapunzel window high in the round tower is carved ANNO CORONATIS MCMIII. I would rate it as Watt's masterpiece if I had to choose one.

1902 also saw the building of the Ruskin Recreation Rooms in town. This building at the top corner of Drury Lane finishes off the laundry complex. The name indicates Watt's admiration for Ruskin and his determination to follow the great man in seeking to better the working classes by providing wholesome recreation and improving instruction.

Let every dawn of morning
be to you as the remains of
life and every setting sun
be to you as its close. RUSKIN

is carved over the carriage arch leading to the laundry, a sentiment which I find not at all helpful or meaningful. On the Drury Lane side is

THEY SAY
WHAT SAY THEY
DO YE WELL
AND LET THEM SAY

which is perhaps a useful guide in life.

At Lake House and the Ruskin Rooms there is a demonstrative use of reclaimed materials, in fact the reclaimed materials to some extent have determined their designs. Having obtained some curved pediments from somewhere for instance, he had to build either a curved bay or a round tower. It seems as though Richard Watt sorted through a pile of bits of old carved stone, a job lot of salvaged windows and some doors and flooring, musing "what can I make out of this lot?" rather than sitting at a drawing board with a piece of blank paper and actually designing it. In fact by 1902 he had established a yard in town for doing just that, complete with a pair of houses called Cranford Gardens dated 1903, one of his nicest Italian compositions, one being for his clerk of works Mr Entwistle.

After the death of Walter Aston, who was perhaps his best collaborator, he took on W Longworth who was this time by contract, not an architect but simply a draftsman. A string of five further villas followed in 1905-6.

High Morland and Aldwarden Hill are the biggest; both now subdivided. The motor house to High Morland stands right on the road and is, together with the Aosta gateway next door,

the most strikingly crazy feature to the casual passer-by of the whole ensemble. This is where it becomes apparent that Watt is deliberately setting one house against another in one big composition, sometimes adding a feature to one house that is particularly effective from next door, or that serves visually to tie two houses together.

In front of Aldwarden Hill however is a little Doric Lodge which is an anomaly, for this is the only time he re-erected an entire building without playing with it. It comes from the Royal Infirmary in Manchester which once occupied the whole of the Piccadilly Gardens site.

At Chantry Dane he incorporated a huge Ionic portico at the back, which was far too big for the building, necessitating some very awkward manoeuvres on the first floor where it intruded into the house. It has been removed although its plinth remains; perhaps it started to slide down the hill. I think it is likely that it came from the old Manchester Museum that was demolished to build the YMCA building of 1909.

Over the kitchen window at the front is inscribed

IF SOLID HAPPINESS WE PRIZE.
WITHIN OUR GRASP THIS JEWEL LIES;
　AND THEY ARE FOOLS WHO ROAM:
THE WORLD HAS NOTHING TO BESTOW;
FROM OUR OWN SELVES OUR JOYS MUST FLOW,
　AND THAT DEAR HUT, OUR HOME

Chantry Dane, like White Howe, is stretched

out to look much bigger than it really is. Even so HUT is something of an understatement.

Broad Terraces is an outrageous design, overloaded with salvaged bits. I like it a lot, it is very bold. Here we can see at its most extreme the particular way in which Richard Watt used old materials. He favoured bits from classical buildings. Classical buildings have a rigid system of proportion of the parts to the whole. He ignored this, incorporating them into a building which is far too small for its parts. One result of this is that his houses, especially this one, are greatly over-windowed by the standards of the time. They are also very bold and sculptural. The Roman pantiles have the same effect because as well as being sculptural they are individually much bigger than common tiles or slates; he liked especially to use them on very small bits of roof. The over-windowing is a very un-Italian effect although good for England, showing that Watt's houses are by no means a straight crib.

Broad Terraces bears two inscriptions. At the side is
THERE'S A DIVINITY THAT SHAPES OUR ENDS
ROUGH HEW THEM HOW WE WILL
which is from Hamlet. Over the kitchen window facing the road is
LE VRAI EST LE SEUL BEAU

The interior is vintage Watt with some good internal vistas and lighting effects between the two staircases. A recent owner has sought to out-Watt Watt by opening it up between floors, decorating throughout in a zany antique style, and adding some new inscriptions, such as:-
OGNI SPERANTA VOI CH'ENTRATA LASCIATE 1990
on a brass roundel in the hall floor, and
DU SUBLIME AU RIDICULE IL N'Y A QU'UN PAS
round the walls.

The Round House which ends the series is at first sight a joke for it is emphatically square. The gatepiers are the clue, for one is indeed square but the other is round. Sure enough the square block is matched by a round tower which dominates the garden but is scarcely visible from the road. The two are linked by a flat-roofed section in a manner reminiscent of Lake House, but the geometry is complicated further by a square bay set diagonally at the join - made of reclaimed materials of course - and by the way the whole house is set at a canted angle to the road.

The Round House has a particularly charming building in its garden. It is hard to know what it was for. Its main purpose appears to be to provide a good nesting site for nuthatches. They live in the tiny cupola which tops a sort of upside-down cabbage on legs. Watt was a great bird-lover, not only providing perches and nesting-places for birds on all of his buildings but also the communal wilderness at the bottom of the gardens called - by him I suspect - Sanctuary Moor.

Richard Watt finally married in 1906, aged 64. His wife disapproved of his extravagant building activities, which ceased forthwith.

There was to be one last building however, his best known, and one last partially-realised scheme.

The Belle Epoque punctuates King Street. The tall narrow tower is the single most prominent landmark. Window shoppers stop and stare. Tourists read the list of English Kings on the octagonal pillar uncomprehendingly. Some might take the time to puzzle out the improving quotes carved around the tiny front yard:-

Our Noble King Alfred the Great
his last words
... COMFORT THE POOR
PROTECT AND SHELTER THE WEAK,
AND WITH ALL THY MIGHT
RIGHT THAT WHICH IS WRONG
THEN SHALL THE LORD LOVE THEE
AND GOD HIMSELF SHALL BE THY GREAT
REWARD.
AD 849   Aetat 53   AD 901

The tower was intended as a personal memorial to Elizabeth Gaskell, whose works Richard Watt admired. The rest was the King's Coffee House. This was another effort at social engineering but offered to the whole town, unlike the Ruskin Rooms. The intention was to tempt the townsfolk, especially those of the working classes, out of the numerous pubs and into a more wholesome environment where they could consume coffee and buns instead of beer and scratchings, and could read newspapers and journals. It was not a great success. It is ironic that King Street is now dominated by establishments where you can do just that; Watt was ahead of his time.

It is an extraordinary building, very small but extremely eventful. Every stone tells a story - they are all different, individually outlined, and many carry inscriptions. An odd feature is the change of colour of the tower above head height from the buff Derbyshire sandstone which he usually selected from the demolition yards to a white Portland stone. It looks very odd from the street but I think there was an aesthetic necessity for this: see below. As for where the stone came from, it looks new, and as Portland only started to be used in Manchester in about 1900 I can only suggest it fell off the back of a lorry, perhaps being surplus to requirements when Lloyds Bank at the corner of the Manchester King Street was being built.

The numerous inscriptions have a theme. Apart from the references to Mrs Gaskell which are all on the slender tower, they all elaborate the concept of Kingship or rulership and the responsibilities thereof.

"WE OUGHT IN LIFE TO FOSTER
ALL THAT MAKES GOODNESS EASIER
AND SETS BARRIERS
OF WHATEVER KIND ACROSS THE FLOWERY
WAYS OF SIN"
            WILLm EWART GLADSTONE
to which carved quote is appended in very small letters
'Do not these words epitomise
those eloquent appeals

& that strenuous life
of the Grand Old Man?'

I feel sure that the little appendage says more about Watt than Gladstone.

There is some notable salvage. Under the carriage arch, deeply shaded where it can hardly be seen, is a wonderfully exotic hanging lamp, which can only be Italian and Baroque. It would look good on the set of a Mozart opera.

ΠH
Sun Morn 18 June 2000
v. hard to see
Belle Epoque

Behind are two enormous Doric columns. Watt initially hoped these would be on the street corner but for once the town council demurred. So he has had to park them at the back, supporting nothing in particular. They come from the grand classical church of St Peter's in Manchester which was demolished, following the flight of most of its congregation to places like Knutsford, in 1907. The church stood where the trams stop now in St Peter's Square; a Portland stone cross marks the spot. Behind the columns are two huge and decaying wooden wheels which are reputed to have been used to transport the columns and to have been simply abandoned here when the job was done. Each column is made up of four drums, so that is eight journeys. I hope it was only from the railway yard, not all the way from Manchester.

Swinton Square is the last job to be considered here although it is actually dated on its diminutive white tower E(crown)R AD 1902. Underneath in very worn letters is CORONATION SQUARE, but this name is little used. It is a modest job in itself but important to a much larger picture which with the building of the Gaskell Memorial Tower was now complete.

There are different sorts of architectural pleasures. One is that given by a single building of great beauty or subtlety or power - or curiosity, like the Belle Epoque. Pleasure of a different order is to be had from a whole group of buildings artfully disposed in a landscape or a townscape. Here it is the changing relationships between the buildings as you perambulate around them which provide the enjoyment, the way one building answers another; like a set of variations upon a theme. Such a pleasure is to be had in the City of London by going round the Wren churches, although one is always aware of how much has been lost or spoiled.

The whole can be so much greater than the sum of its parts. This is the secret of a place like Blaise Hamlet near Bristol, or a landscape like Stourhead in Wiltshire, both seminal creations of the Picturesque movement.

Watt's eight villas on Legh Road work on this principle. Each one is entertaining in itself, but it is the relationship between them that provides the greatest pleasure. That is why there are so many outbuildings. The garden temples and motor houses and water towers serve to connect up and set off the houses. The walk along Legh Road was clearly intended as a visual treat, or a whole series of visual treats, which it still is. So was the walk along Toft Road but this is largely hidden by trees today.

The comparison with Blaise Hamlet and Stourhead can be taken further. Blaise was the work of a professional architect, Nash, and was essentially conceived on paper. But Stourhead was the work of an amateur, the banker Henry Hoare, and was conceived, bit by bit, during innumerable walks and rides - adding a bit here, taking a bit away there, adjusting this, adding a new accent there, just so, to create a great work of art in the aggregate, to be enjoyed just as it was created. This was the way Watt worked; not on paper but on the spot, not all at once in a flash of genius but bit by bit and with much tinkering. Maddening for his contractors - one is reputed to have met him at the station with a gun - but highly successful in the end.

It is harder to appreciate that Watt planned and achieved a similar effect for the whole town of Knutsford. What audacity the man had!

In order to achieve a grand landscape effect on a large scale it is not always necessary to own or control a lot of land. It can be done by judiciously buying up a bit here and a bit there and building your eyecatchers on them as though all the land in between was yours as well. This was the trick that Repton used at Attingham, Shropshire, where he built a lodge on the far side of the A5, so suggesting that the road went through a vast park, not round a modest one. Randle Wilbraham of Rode Hall had done the same thing in 1754 when he built the sham castle on top of Mow Cop.

So Watt, having created his spectacular bit of townscape in the laundry on Drury Lane, realised that by building an eyecatcher there at the other end of the town in the same dazzling style, and by placing a tall accent in between, and especially if a unifying landscape could be created in front, a much bigger picture could be made. So the little white tower of Swinton Square answers the stacked towers and minarets of the laundry at the other end, and the slender tower of the Belle Epoque rising above the rooftops provides the linking accent. It would never have worked in Cheshire brick. The effect depended on their dazzling whiteness catching the eye and the jumbled houses and rooftops of the town fading into the background. That is why the top of the Belle Epoque tower had to be white, and why it had to be so tall.

In the foreground was the rough wetland of the Moor. Watt had ambitious plans for this, but in the event the simple landscaping with open water and mown grass suffices to tie the whole together.

It was all designed to be seen from the railway embankment, and indeed it has been recorded how spectacular Knutsford looked to passengers, including Richard Watt himself of course, approaching from Manchester. More's the pity therefore that, although most of the elements of the composition are still there, they have lost all coherence because the laundry has lost its topknots.

It was delight in the changing landscape effects of his own creations that killed Richard Harding Watt. He used to stand up in his carriage to enjoy his works; one day in 1913 the horse shied and he fell and was killed. What a way to go.

Watt's sources

Watt's buildings are so exotic that it is natural to seek the sources of his inspiration far away in exotic places. The Italian connection is obvious, and sometimes overt like the gateway in Legh Road that he copied from one in Aosta in the Italian Alps. His sketchbooks reveal prototypes from further afield - the gate tower in Damascus that inspired the laundry's watertower, even the towers and balconies of Australian colonial houses. Likewise it is tempting to compare him with the most exotic and progressive of his contemporaries - Charles Rennie Macintosh, or Edgar Wood or Voysey. There are parallels, and he was probably aware of the work of all three - two of Miss Cranston's tea-rooms, showcases for the Macintosh style, were a short stroll from Watt's Glasgow office for example.

Surprisingly however, Knutsford itself may have provided many of his ideas. Local prototypes can be found for many of his themes, although he always used them in his own unique way.

Take brickwork. Watt's walls are never plain and flat. He liked to use his materials interestingly, with some bricks recessed or standing proud to give light and shade. There are plenty of older buildings in Knutsford that do just this, like the group of Antrobus houses in King Street opposite the George. Brickies have liked to do it since bricks were invented. It is a local characteristic.

He liked inscriptions of an improving nature. This is an unusual feature in any age, but as it happens he only had to look across from the end of Legh Road at Higher Town Post Office of 1881, decorated with pastoral scenes and mottoes in plaster:-

THINK	NO
OF EASE	GAINS
BUT	WITHOUT
WORK ON	PAINS

Our mission is to sell
yours to quickly buy

We'll do our part full well
if you'll only let us try

What about a really personal quirk of Watt's buildings: the occasional use of a childish smiling face? The Belle Epoque has one, so does Broad Terraces, and there is one in Drury Lane. He didn't have to go far for this idea either: just to the smiley suns in the town hall roof which are such an unexpected feature of that unsmiling building.

A feature that above all marks out Watt's buildings from any other is the random fenestration. His windows do not come in straight rows or simple symmetries, nor in regulation sizes. Even here we can find a prototype on the doorstep. Sit in a pew in the old dissenting chapel on Brook Street and weigh up the strange fenestration of the long wall behind the preacher, as many must have done over the years during long sermons. The windows aren't exactly random, nor are they asymmetrical, but their unusually assorted effect could certainly have provided Watt with food for thought.

Watt Style?

The work of Richard Harding Watt at Knutsford is so odd that we cannot expect him to have had any general influence. Nevertheless his spirit has been rekindled here and there. The obvious parallel is Portmeirion. This, the dream creation of Clough Williams-Ellis, came a good twenty-five years later but Clough recounts that it existed in his mind for at least that time. Could there be any connection? He would have been about twenty when Watt was creating his fantasy world at Knutsford. Clough Williams-Ellis's dream took on a greater urgency during the First World War. He recounts 'Throughout the years of my war service abroad I had to dream of something other than the horror, destruction and savagery - and what more different than to build with whatever serenity, kindness and loveliness one could contrive on some beautiful unknown site ...'. The search for a site was to take him all around the shores and islands of the country - he always visualised his dream village by the sea - only to find the perfect site just five miles from his own home in Merioneth.

Portmeirion was designed on the hoof just like Legh Road and Drury Lane but it sprang much more quickly into life because it was the realisation of a long-held and honed dream. It is more theatrical than Legh Road and practices more deception. Watt's houses may be weird but they are good and solid and what you see is what they are. Portmeirion employs all the tricks of the scenepainter - trompe l'oeil shading, false perspective, buildings with no backs. It all looks wonderful from the right viewpoint but, as in the theatre, it fails if seen from the cheapest seats. Aerial photographs of Portmeirion are particularly cruel. This is why the modern-day makeover of Broad Terraces is not altogether satisfactory; it is much more Portmeirion than Knutsford.

Like Watt, Williams-Ellis was clever at using second-hand materials. Witty too, see his clifftop lookout constructed around a twirly chimneypot, or the temple portico which is really a vast Victorian fireplace. Although entertaining, and in some cases valuable in their own right, the second-hand pieces are not central to the dream; Portmeirion could have been made out of almost anything.

Like Legh Road and Drury Lane it is all very Italianate. And yet Clough Williams-Ellis insisted that it was also Welsh; and Cornish, Japanese, piratical, operatic, Baroque. Watt too was Italianate but, as we have seen, surprisingly rooted in Knutsford itself.

Despite the witticisms and exoticisms Clough's village can be summed up as Sorrento or Portofino in Merioneth; a Mediterranean port transported to Wales. Richard Watt had a slightly different vision; Bellagio or Salo, transported from the Italian lakes to Knutsford. Sanctuary Moor and the pool at the Moor are just sufficiently wet to serve, for the purposes of the vision, as the shores of Lake Como, or Garda.

The spirit of Richard Harding Watt and of Clough Williams-Ellis is not dead even today. The one-horse town of Cheadle in Staffordshire is famous for just one building, Pugin's masterwork St Giles. But a mile outside town on the Oakamoor Road is another in the making, or a dreadful eyesore depending on your point of view.

LES + MAVE is the unlikely message woven into the roof tiles of a big group of buildings resembling, with their wide doors and wooden cupolas, a stableyard. What are they? Their date and purpose should be given by the datestones and inscriptions prominently mounted in the walls, but when a single building has thirteen different datestones and six different dedications, not to mention a whole row of conflicting street names, what are we to think?

In fact it is all new, the inspired creation of Les Oakes, demolition and reclamation a speciality. Its purpose is to house more of the same, for each building is crammed to eye-popping point with salvage and junk of every conceivable kind. The buildings are a kind of permanent exhibition, justifying themselves by preserving and displaying fragments from other buildings that are gone. Not so different from the Burrell really. There is no theme here, no dream, just a fantastic collection fantastically displayed.

It takes a special kind of person to take a pile of fragments from demolished buildings and visualise what can be made of them; and then to realise the vision, because second-hand stones are hugely heavy but horribly fragile, and because there is something fundamentally unrespectable about re-using other people's castoffs. Each has done it in their own particular way. The results in all three cases may indeed be somewhat raffish but the world would be a poorer place without them.

No. 53   THE MOOR, SHOWING KNUTSFORD FROM THE RAILWAY

The Moor and Knutsford
from the railway
   Courtesy Moira Stevens

THE TERRACE TOWERS.   KNUTSFORD.

Terrace Towers.
   Courtesy Moira Stevens

e Belle Epoch's smiley
or

right: 1907 May Queen
Courtesy Joan Leach

yline and Minaret
Courtesy Joan Leach

The Tower.
Courtesy Joan Le

The Ruskin Rooms in 19

Autl

76 photographs taken by
e author showing the
askell Tower from the
oor - an impossible view
day - and the Drury
ne minaret still standing,
t without its conical
of.

utsford. This wonderful
cture of the Legh Road
yline across Sanctuary
oor is preserved in the
rary.

Courtesy Cheshire County
Council

Above left: Portrait of Richard Harding Watt

Above right: Watt sketch entitled 'Alterations to Croft'

Watt's own house, The Croft, as published in 'The Builder'.

Courtesy Joan Lead

Morning at Croft

tile House

Morning at the Croft.
KNUTSFORD — 29/4/12

An Hour with Mozart -th
Croft interior?

warden Gate and plan.

nutsford garden gate - or
it the prototype at
osta?

King street — Knutsford.

Coffee House

Gaskell oeuvres list - prepared for the stonemason - later to appear on the Gaskell Tower

skell conundrum -

etch: Proposed Post Office
Courtesy Joan Leach

Gateway at Salo

Lakeside, Cadenabbia

The Landing at (by the Hotel Bellevue) Cadenabbia.
Lago di Como.

S. Caterina del Sasso.
on Lake Maggiore.

S.Caterina del Sasso

Maggiore —.   on road from Bouvino. to Stresa
Friday. 27/4 06.

Bullock cart. Could this
have been the inspiration
for Drury Lane?

…att's impact on the
…utsford skyline.

View of the Round House from Broad Terraces.

Below: White Howe

White Howe

17 June 2000 D* Terrace steps

gh Road Scene, with the
sta gate and High
orland Lodge.

e diminutive tower of
vinton Square, which
swers to the Drury Lane
oup at the other end of
e Moor.

LAKE HOUSE

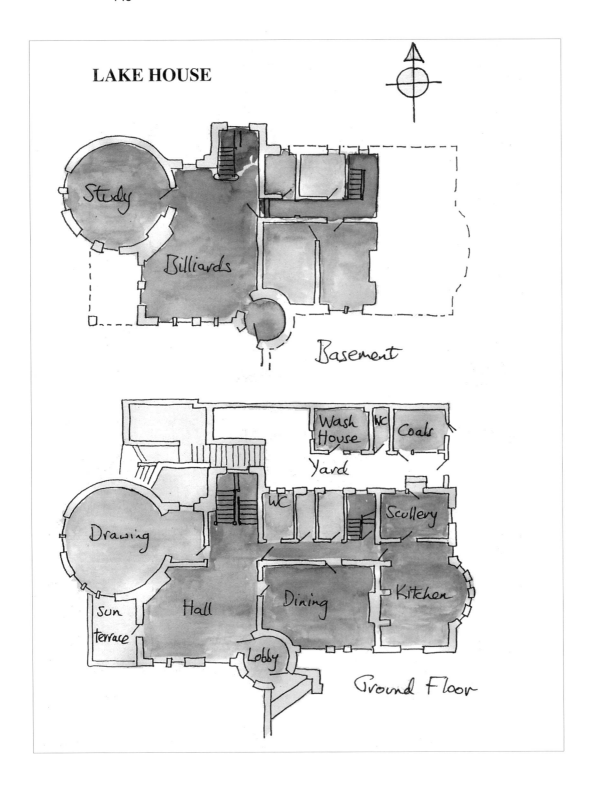

Study

Billiards

Basement

Wash House

WC

Coals

Yard

WC

Scullery

Drawing

Sun terrace

Hall

Dining

Kitchen

Lobby

Ground Floor

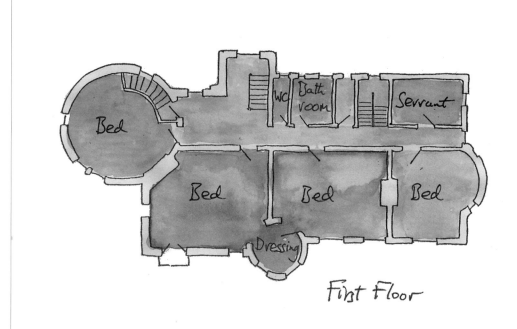

First Floor

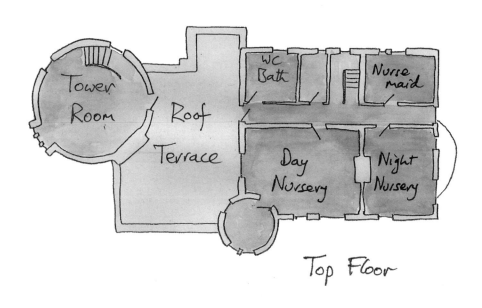

Top Floor

Details of Lake House

Lake House and Sanctuary Moor.

The garden of Lake House.

Chantry Dane Water Tower fed off the roof. The arch frames an arche tower on top of the garden shed which was p there for that very purpose.

Chantry Dane - wooden bell which hung in the belfry seen opposite.

Chantry Dane nursery or the top floor, with a little balcony under the eaves and eye-catching roof ligh made possible by glass tiles.

garden in front of
antry Dane. Old
otographs show that
ere was a giant Ionic
tio here - see page 55.

e bird house/garden
ed of Chantry Dane
kes a pleasant eye-
tcher from the
ighbouring gardens.

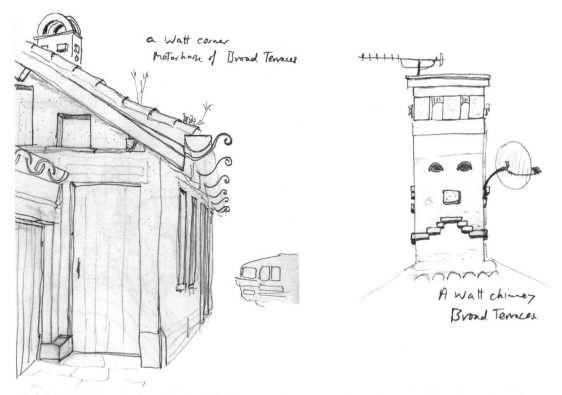

a Watt corner
Motorhouse of Broad Terraces

A Watt chimney
Broad Terraces

The Round House which is
not mis-named although it
appears to be so from the
road. Note the square and
round gate piers which
anticipate the house
design.

Broad Terraces is perhaps Watt's boldest house, and it has undergone some equally bold interior surgery in recent times.

The Doric Lodge in front of Aldwarden Hill is a complete building re-erected. Only the chimney betrays the Watt influence

The Doric Lodge in its original position by Manchester Royal Infirmary is seen here on the far right of a view of 1860.

e site of Watt's office in
anchester, on Piccadilly
rdens. It is pleasing that
e replacement building, a
ffee and tea house of
out 1912, is Moorish in
le but the gold dome is
photographer's trick
rrowed from the next
eet.

he Old Manchester
useum on Peter Sreet in
anchester. I think Watt
ed the columns again at
hantry Dane (see pages
2 -153).

Portmeirion viewpoint, built around a reclaimed twirly chimney pot.
A fake ship on the quay at Portmeirion commemorates Clough Williams-Ellis's own Portmadoc ketch that was lost in a gale.

cene-painting at Portmeirion. The garden
bour is just corrugated iron and paint. The
assical portico is just that - nothing else.

Les Oakes's yard outside Cheadle in Staffordshire is a treasure trove of reclaimed materials and a brilliant demonstration of how they can be used.

Seven
THE LIBRARY

Earlier libraries. Andrew Carnegie - biography, interest in free libraries. Alfred Darbyshire - autobiography, works. The first public library 1904 - librarians - plans for a new library 2000.

Knutsford's little public library when it opened on 31 December 1904 was a source of considerable pride to the town, although as always there were those who labelled it a white elephant.

The town has grown mightily in the intervening century, and so have the information and facilities a library is expected to provide. This is written the very day, 21 June 2000, that the ground is due to be broken for its replacement. Replacing the library however has proved to be even more of a saga than building it in the first place.

There were of course libraries here long before 1904. In the great country houses that surround Knutsford there were, and in some cases still are, extensive and valuable libraries; but access to them was limited to the family and guests, and occasionally trusted servants. In 1839 the Knutsford Working Man's Library opened in the old courtroom on the marketplace. It was a subscription library. 10/6 a year made you an honorary member; lesser mortals paid a penny a week. Even this however could disenfranchise some people; a

poor young man for instance, up-and-coming but penniless.

By 1900 the concept of free public libraries provided on the rates by the local council had become a general one. Councils up and down the country passed resolutions, but the resolution was easier than the action, because land had to be found for a site and capital had to be found for a building.

There was one golden-egg-laying goose who could be applied to for funds, and that was Andrew Carnegie. The story of why a multi-millionaire in Pittsburg, America - he was reputed to be the richest man on earth - would interest himself in the building of a new public library in Knutsford is worth telling.

He was born in a poor weaver's cottage in Dunfermline in 1835. With his family he emigrated to America in 1848, arriving penniless at Allegheny, by Pittsburg, at the age of thirteen. He spent the first half of his life in relentless self-improvement and competitive investment, clawing his way always upwards but steadied and supported by his strong moral sense and by the mutual loyalty of his family and friends. He was the steel king of America, although his burgeoning wealth was due more to shrewd investment than manufacture.

In 1868, just twenty years after his arrival in the New World, he wrote an astonishing policy statement for himself:-
'Thirty-three and an income of $50,000 per annum ... beyond this never earn - make no effort to increase fortune but spend surplus each year for benevolent purposes.'

The benevolent spending of the surplus occupied him increasingly for the rest of his life. Getting rid of money is not a major problem to most people, but after he retired from business in 1901 his investments were earning money at such a phenomenal rate that in spite of all his efforts to give it away he got richer than ever. In 1910 he entrusted the great bulk of the remainder, $125,000,000, to a body whose job it was to do what he had been unable to do on his own: give it away.

First to benefit were his twin home towns, Dunfermline and Pittsburg, but over the years of the beneficence of Andrew Carnegie and of the Carnegie Trust has sponsored many and various projects world-wide. The name Carnegie turns up in some surprising places, from the credits of the brilliant children's' TV programme 'Sesame Street', called the longest street in the world because it has reached almost every country, to a discreet plaque on the organ at St Paul's church, Macclesfield, where no-one could see it except the grateful organist.

Libraries were a favourite project. He remembered his young self, a telegraph messenger boy with no money but thirsting for knowledge, in a city where there was no public library. A retired manufacturer named Colonel Anderson made his own private library available to working boys, such as he himself had been; but there was a charge of two dollars a year. Even this was impossible for the Carnegie family. The Colonel was prepared to put aside the annual fee in the case of bound apprentices, but young Andrew did not qualify for the rebate. He decided to protest in print - not for the last time - which had the desired effect of a change in the rules. '*To him* (Colonel Anderson) *I owe a taste for literature which I would not exchange for all the millions that were ever amassed by man*' he wrote, and it is indirectly to him, for Andrew Carnegie was a man who never forgot a good turn, that we owe all the Carnegie libraries in the world, from the huge Carnegie Library of Pittsburgh - "*Free to the People*" it proclaims at the top of their website, as it does in stone over the door - to our own here in Knutsford.

Andrew Carnegie was not a man who liked to make things too easy. Self-help was his creed, not lie back and be fed. He vetted all the applications personally, querying them on design grounds as well as financial ones. Alderman Fletcher Moss has described his own fight for a public library in Didsbury (in 'Fifty Years of Public Work in Didsbury' 1915). It was certainly not a matter of asking for the money and waiting for the cheque to arrive. Alderman Moss and the chief librarian were able to arrange a brief meeting with the great man, finding him brusque but genial. Photographs show him a dapper little man, notably bright-eyed and bushy-tailed. Carnegie, like William Lever to whom he bears many resemblances, was jealous of anything that wasted time, even seconds; Carnegie even to the extent of inventing his own speling that omited al unecesary leters.

There are more than 2,500 Carnegie Free Public Libraries in the world. They cost him at least $56,000,000. I have no doubt that Andrew Carnegie considered the money well spent, and if it were possible to quantify the benefits it was probably the best investment he ever made.

By 1902 Knutsford Council had secured £1,500 from Mr Carnegie for a building, but was still without a site. Carnegie never paid for the site for a new library, thus ensuring that the local community had to make an effort at the start. 'When the library is supported by the community all taint of charity is dispelled' he said. In 1904 Mr Holt of The Grove gave a plot opposite the old Brook Street Chapel - whose site had been given by a previous owner of the Grove, Isaac Antrobus - and work could begin.

The architect chosen to design the new library was Alfred Darbyshire, of Rockford Lodge in Manor Park, near the library site, where he had lived since 1895.

'A dizzy, inconsequential figure blowing in the winds of fashion' is one opinion of Alfred Darbyshire. 'One of Manchester's cherished possessions, a man of fine brain, and with a heart of gold' is another. Let Mr Darbyshire speak for himself:-

'I was born at No. 8, Peru Street, Salford, on the 20th of June, 1839.

My parents were members of the Society of Friends, commonly called the Quakers. The family removed from the terrace in which I was born into Peel Street, adjacent to that sombre and severely classic edifice, St Philip's Church. Here, whilst amusing my infantile self in a sort of treadmill fashion on the front door steps, I fell onto the nosing of the topmost one, and just escaped a fractured skull. The brand of this mishap still remains. I do not remember whether I was considered a child of beauty or not; but if I was this catastrophe effectually obliterated all claims to good looks, and left me a plain-looking youngster.' (the quotes are from his 'An Architect's experiences: Professional, Artistic, and Theatrical.' written at Manor Park, Knutsford, Cheshire in 1897)

Mr Darbyshire's reminiscences of his experiences are much more theatrical than artistic or architectural; in fact it is what we might today call a "luvvie" book. Names are dropped, opening nights and fancy dress parties are described in great detail, and reviews quoted verbatim. Mr Darbyshire was a clubable man, by his own account at the centre of an artistic milieu of a city that one might assume didn't have one. It gradually becomes clear on reading the book that both the assessments of the man quoted above are perfectly true.

In 1851 he was sent to the Quaker School at Ackworth in Yorkshire, but '*I suppose the fascinating influence of art caused a neglect of other studies; at all events I was sent to another school, Lindow Grove Academy, at Alderley, in Cheshire, to finish my education. I plunged into the classics, modern languages, and mathematics under the learned Dr Satterthwaite.*' The Academy was housed in a large building on the main road between Alderley Edge and Wilmslow. Recently rescued from spectacular dereliction it is currently - what else? - a cafe bar. Dr Satterthwaite lived nearby in a plain white house, and is buried under a no-frills stone in front of the Quaker meeting house in Wilmslow. Alfred Darbyshire must always have been a trial to the Society of Friends, leaning towards everything that they abhorred. A career as an artist would have been considered by them to be immorally frivolous, but '*Notwithstanding the warnings received, and suggestions made of probable failure, I determined to try my fate in the world of art.*'

In the end Alfred Darbyshire was ejected from the Society of Friends, which is rather sad for both parties I think.

He describes the start of his architectural career:-
'*On the 31st of October, 1855, I was duly and legally articled to an architect in Manchester. My master [Mr. P.B. Alley] had been in partnership with Mr Richard Lane, the leading architect of the town and district; and the firm of Lane and Alley had a touch of humour in it which certainly did not suggest genius or high art. In spite of the unpoetic title of the firm, it was the local centre of classical thought. Mr Lane was a gentleman and a scholar. His practice was almost exclusively devoted to an attempt to force upon a commercial nineteenth-century town, with a humid and sunless climate, the refinement and perfect beauty of the art of the Greeks in the golden age of Pericles.*'

What a splendid sentence that last one is! A devastating critique of revived classicism in Manchester, indicative of a change of fashion towards the gothic. The demolition of unfashionable classical buildings in Manchester, encouraged by such criticism, was to provide Richard Harding Watt of Knutsford with his raw materials at just the time that Alfred Darbyshire's library was being built. Sadly however it is the only time in the whole book that Mr Darbyshire ventures any such rigour; the rest is but gush. I shall give an example at this point :-

"The Artist's Ball"
'*My last sight of Randolph Caldecott was at the Grand Costume Ball held at the Prince's Hall, Piccadilly, on the 19th of May, 1855. He was my introducer, and I still treasure the beautiful ticket designed by Walter Crane and signed by Caldecott. What a wonderful gathering of Royalty, artists, and literary people that Ball brought together. The tableaux were explained by Forbes Robertson in verse entitled "the Masque of Painters". written by Edmund Gosse; and constituted perfect pictures, arranged by some of the most celebrated painters*

of the time. I elected to represent a nobleman of the "Renaissance", and so enthusiastic was everybody for truth to history and period that I had a "Garter" collar with a George pendant, made in Paris strictly in accordance with the Statute of the Noble Order as laid down by Henry VIII; the garter itself was studded with the finest paste diamonds obtainable in London. I wore a real rapier of the period; also a beautiful pouch dagger of German make of the time of Maximilian. My "get-up" was voted a success; I had to be photographed by electric light for the album given to the Princess of Wales as a memento of an event unique in the history "Fancy Dress" balls.'

Perhaps we can understand after all why he and the Quakers did not see eye to eye.

After setting up in practice as an architect in 1862, his first significant job was at Lyme. Here he completed the stone conservatory by Lewis Wyatt, and built a large and hideous stable block on the hill above the mansion.

Darbyshire was forever moving house. '*In the year 1871, I built my own house in Broughton Park, on the outskirts of Manchester. I entered into this piece of extravagance for two reasons. In the first place I wanted to give expression to a few fanciful notions I had with regard to domestic architecture, and which I felt no client would ever be induced to allow me to realise; in the second place I thought what might be looked upon as architectural eccentricities would arouse some criticism and draw the attention of the public to the fact that a young and struggling architect must advertise in some form in order to live.*' As Cecil

Stewart writes in his 'Stones of Manchester', '*a confessed rogue indeed!*'.

One of his roguish jobs was the construction of lodges and gates for the new Alexandra Park in Mosside. '*It is difficult to imagine how such a simple problem as this lodge could result in such a complex structure.*' (Cecil Stewart again) '*There is a clock tower over the entrance, with bits of timber-framing in the upper portions, and a steep, chateau-like roof. There are tall Elizabethan chimneys which sprout out of the irregular hipped and gabled roof at the most surprising places. Bands of encaustic tiles divide the first floor from the second and enrich the tower; there are stone dressings here and there, and an elaborate cornice at the eaves contrived of bricks laid edgeways and anglewise and corbelled. It may have been thought picturesque; it was certainly called 'pretty'; but no-one could say that it represented a contribution to the development of architecture.*'

Alfred Darbyshire did however make one significant contribution to architecture, and public safety, and that was in the design of theatres. Theatres were deathtraps. The combination of hot lights, gas, inflammable scenery, darkness and lots of people was, in the modern phrase, a disaster waiting to happen. When it did, as at Exeter on the 5 September 1887, the violent through draught set in motion by the fire and the panic of people unable to find a way out made sure it was a really bad one.

The Irving-Darbyshire safety plan of 1884

was the result of parallel thinking and then collaboration between those two gentlemen. The plan directed that theatres be made as fireproof as possible, especially the staircases and passageways which are completely so; clearly marked exits are provided for every part of the auditorium, as there are also for the dressing rooms. The building is to be isolated from all surrounding buildings. And the stage can be instantly sealed from the auditorium by a fire curtain; the showing of this curtain during every performance is Alfred Darbyshire's best epitaph.

So although his Palace of Varieties theatre in Manchester looked like the most outrageous confection - a later and a duller age has stripped it of all its exterior finery - it concealed a serious purpose and was a considerable landmark in the design of all theatres and auditoria.

The library at Knutsford is a relatively tame example of Darbyshire's architecture, but is nevertheless remarkably forceful for its diminutive size. Carnegie specified that a library should have separate reference, children's and lending departments. On the smallest possible scale Knutsford library has all three, each under a separate bit of roof and clearly identifiable from the outside. The reference room is the largest and is lit by a large oriel facing Adam's Hill and by runs of dormers on each side like those of the Methodist church. To the right is the lower children's room and in the angle between them, behind the porch, the lending section. The front is decorated by a modest amount of yellow terracotta, declaring to the world that this is indeed the Free Public Library and that its date is 1904.

It was changed very little from the architect's first plan of 1903, and it has changed remarkably little since. The glass turret over the lending desk never was built, and the oriel ended up square not round. The railings have gone. A room has been added at the back which is now the reference section and a cellar excavated beneath.

The first librarian was the Rev G A Payne, Minister of the Unitarian Chapel across the road. Rev Payne served as librarian until 1930, at a starting salary of £20 per annum, for which sum he was expected to be on duty from 7am to 9.30pm.

As Minister of the chapel he was a successor at two removes of Henry Green, author of 'Knutsford; its Traditions and History' of 1859. Henry Green's book is the primary source on Knutsford, but it is very difficult to find what you want. In fairness to the Reverend gentleman that work was initially a series of lectures. This book, I fear, will suffer from the same fault. But it does have pictures.

After half a century the Carnegie Library of Knutsford was outgrowing its building and plans were made for its replacement. That's right, half a century. It has taken another half century for anything to happen. A report of of 1947 recommended that the Sessions House should be earmarked for a new library. In 1973 it was proposed instead to have a completely new building in the middle of Stanley Park, where Booth's car park is now. A design was prepared by the County Council who were now responsible for libraries and a tender was accepted at £160,000. It would have been square, concrete, large-windowed and flat-roofed, like Wilmslow library or Marple, but nothing happened. Now in 2000 the Sessions House may not be in use as a Crown Court for much longer, but the new-build option is still the preferred one. Squareness, concrete, large windows and flat roofs we may safely guess however, without having seen the plans, are out!

Will Mr Carnegie's and Mr Darbyshire's library make its centenary?

Alfred Darbyshire

The first design.

...racotta round the
...trance.

...e finished result.

OUR ANGEL OF PEACE

Cartoons of Andrew Carnegie lampoon his vow poverty, his propensity to build libraries and his promotion of world peace.

Andrew Carnegie
*Courtesy Knutsford Library
and Cheshire County Council*

Some of Alfred Derbyshire's works were outrageous: the lodge and gates to Alexandra Park and the Palace Theatre - now, alas. stripped of its exterior finery.

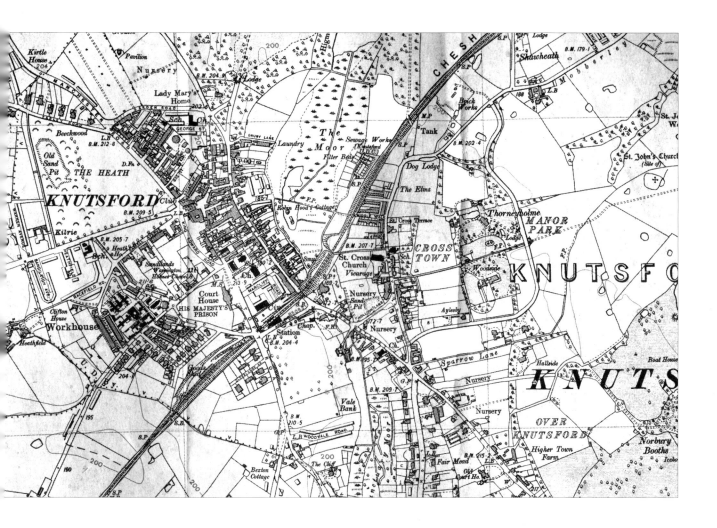